THE ELK HUNTER'S COOKBOOK

A collection of favorite recipes from members of the Rocky Mountain Elk Foundation

FALCON™

Helena, Montana

ROCKY MOUNTAIN
ELK FOUNDATION

ISBN: 1-56044-301-4

Library of Congress Catalog Card Number: 94-061224

Printed in the United States of America

Falcon Press Publishing Co., Inc.
P.O. Box 1718
Helena, Montana 59624
1-800-582-2665

TABLE OF CONTENTS

About the Rocky Mountain Elk Foundation

Thanks to all Elk Foundation members who submitted recipes for *The Elk Hunter's Cookbook*. Special thanks to Linda Ward for seasoning the project with her wisdom.

The Rocky Mountain Elk Foundation is an international, nonprofit conservation organization. Founded in 1984, the Missoula-based foundation now has more than 85,000 members in 50 states and 23 countries. Through local fundraisers, those members have helped generate $30 million to conserve and enhance 1.5 million acres of critical habitat for elk and other wildlife. These projects and acquisitions include habitat enhancements, management studies, research, conservation education, and hunting heritage programs.

The mission of the Rocky Mountain Elk Foundation is to ensure the future of elk, other wildlife, and their habitat by:

• Conserving, restoring, and enhancing natural habitats;

• Promoting the sound management of wild free-ranging elk, other wildlife, and their habitat;

• Fostering cooperation among federal, state, and private organizations and individuals in wildlife management and habitat conservation; and

• Educating members and the public about habitat conservation, the value of hunting, hunting ethics, and wildlife management.

To learn more about how the Elk Foundation is working for wildlife, please call 1-800-CALL ELK.

Stoking Up Prodigiously

These recipes would have suited Theodore Roosevelt's tastes well. When Roosevelt set out from camp for two or three days' hunting, he carried only a loaf of frying pan bread or perhaps an elk tongue. But when he sat down at a table, Roosevelt could easily devour a whole chicken or half a suckling pig. His friend Lloyd Griscom described Roosevelt's gormandizing as "stoking up prodigiously—as though he were a machine." Theodore Roosevelt Jr. allowed as how his father's coffee cup "was more in the nature of a bathtub." Of course, the tradition of packing only the most spartan fare in the field—and gorging after a hard day's hunt—began long before Teddy Roosevelt stalked the Rockies. May it endure among hunters for generations to come.

Some of the recipes in *The Elk Hunter's Cookbook* create treats light and simple enough to slip into a fanny pack. But most of the dishes set forth on these pages could star in the kind of gastronomic fantasy you might entertain while slogging downslope toward a cold tent, long after dark, some October night.

Though few of us get to hunt elk for more than a week or two each fall, we are elk hunters throughout the year. Our appetites for elk country, for hunting, and for the elk themselves remain undiminished. Savoring the kind of hearty meal we might eat in elk camp—or at least dream about while gnawing on a piece of jerky—is a fine way to keep those appetites keen. So we asked 85,000 friends of ours if they knew any good recipes.

All the recipes in this book come from people who love elk and elk country—every one a member of the Rocky Mountain Elk Foundation. They shared these dishes in the spirit you might swap tall tales and favorite recipes over a low cooking fire. We at the Elk Foundation hope a few of these recipes will find their way into your elk camp. We hope you'll cook them at home, too—and the aromas will carry you back to a dawn at timberline, with three inches of fresh snow . . . Most of all, we hope they will make you want to stoke up prodigiously.

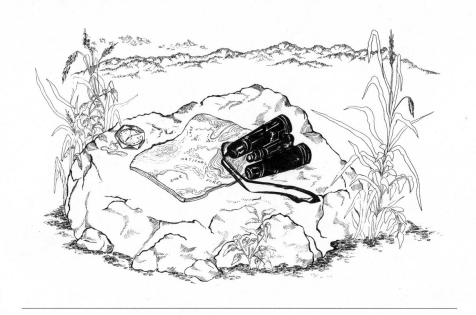

APPETIZERS
AND SOUPS

Elk Party Turnovers

1 envelope dry onion
  soup mix
1 cup shredded cheddar
  cheese
1 lb. ground elk meat
3 pkgs. refrigerated
  crescent rolls

In a medium skillet combine onion soup mix and meat; brown well. Drain off fat, blend in cheese, remove from heat. Separate crescent rolls according to package directions. Cut in half. Place a spoonful of elk mixture in center of each triangle; fold and seal. Place on cookie sheet and bake at 375 degrees for 15 minutes until brown.

Sometimes I partially bake the above for about 10 minutes and freeze them to use later. I have also used boar sausage in the above recipe. Delicious!!! This appetizer goes really quickly at a party. Makes 48.

Margaret C. Robinson
Pelham, New Hampshire

Turkey Roll Ups

**2 lbs. cooked turkey,
sliced ¹/₁₆-inch thick**
**1 can cranberry sauce
(16 oz.)**
**8 oz. cream cheese,
softened**
**6-8 green onions,
chopped**

Mix together cream cheese and green onions. Spread thin amount of cream cheese mixture on turkey slice. Spread thin amount of cranberry sauce on top. Roll up and refrigerate. Cut in 1-inch sections and put toothpicks in them. Serves 20-25.

Cindi Bratvoid
Hamilton, Montana

Tortilla Treat

12 flour tortillas
8 oz. cream cheese
**1 small can chopped
black olives (6 oz.)**
Garlic powder
Onion powder
Salsa or taco sauce

Cream cheese should be at room temperature. Beat cream cheese until soft and smooth. Add a drop of milk to make creamy. Add black olives, garlic, onion powder to taste. Spread this mixture on tortillas and roll them up. Refrigerate 2 or more hours. Slice each tortilla into 8 pieces. Fasten with toothpicks. Serve with taco sauce or salsa. Makes 96.

Sharon Robertson
Kansas City, Kansas

Shrimp Dip

16 oz. cream cheese
1 can diced green chilies,
    drained (4.5 oz.)
1 diced tomato
1 small diced onion
Pickled jalapeños to
    taste, chopped
¹/₂ lb. cooked shrimp or
    crab meat

Warm cheese in double boiler (or microwave). When very soft, mix with balance of ingredients. Warm slowly. Serve warm with chips. Makes about 4 cups.

Cheri Eby
Gunnison, Colorado

Luau Bites

10 water chestnuts,
    halved
5 chicken livers,
    quartered
10 slices bacon
¹/₄ cup soy sauce
2 tsp. brown sugar
20 toothpicks, soaked in
    cold water

Wrap one piece each of water chestnuts and chicken liver in a half slice of bacon; fasten with wooden toothpick. Chill in mixture of soy sauce and brown sugar about ¹/₂ hour. Spoon marinade over occasionally. Drain. Broil 3 inches from heat until bacon is crisp, turning once. Makes 20.

Sharon Robertson
Kansas City, Kansas

CHILI CHEESE DIP

16 oz. of your favorite
  chili (canned,
  homemade, or
  otherwise)
8 oz. cream cheese,
  softened

Mix together and microwave on high for 1½ minutes. Take out and stir. Place back in microwave for 2 minutes. Serve with corn chips. Makes about 3 cups.

Barbara Kinne
Olathe, Colorado

STUFFED MUSHROOMS WITH A HEART

1 elk heart
1 tbsp. salt
½ cup butter
½ cup diced red onion
½ tsp. pepper
½ tsp. garlic powder
½ tsp. tarragon
Salt to taste
½ loaf sourdough bread,
  diced
1 cup grated cheddar
  cheese
1 lb. large fresh
  mushrooms without
  stems
Parmesan cheese

Preheat oven to 350 degrees. Soak elk heart 30 minutes in cold water with 1 tbsp. salt; drain and rinse. Cover with water, boil heart for 20 minutes; drain and cool. Skin and discard thin outer layer, then dice, avoiding tough center.

Melt butter and sauté heart, onion, and spices 5 minutes. Add bread and cheddar cheese. Salt to taste. Remove from heat.

Stuff mushroom caps with mixture and sprinkle with Parmesan cheese. Bake on ungreased cookie sheet 30 minutes. Serve warm.

Sandy Seaton
Emigrant, Montana

Smoked Trout Paté

2 cups trout (cooked,
  skinned, boned,
  drained and flaked)
8 oz. cream cheese
2 tbsp. grated onion
1 tbsp. lemon juice
$1/4$ tsp. Liquid Smoke
$1/4$ tsp. salt
2 dashes (or more)
  Tabasco
1 or 2 tsp. horseradish

Combine all ingredients in food processor and process until smooth. Chill several hours. May be shaped in ball or log and rolled in mixture of $1/2$ cup chopped pecans and 2 tbsp. snipped parsley. Serve with crackers. Can substitute canned salmon for trout. Serves 20.

Sue Gooding
Albuquerque, New Mexico

Sausage Ring

2 lbs. bulk hot pork
  sausage
2 eggs
$1 1/2$ cups crushed Ritz
  crackers
16 oz. cream cheese,
  softened
Cilantro, fresh, chopped
  (optional)
Red bell pepper
  (optional)
Green bell pepper
  (optional)
Yellow bell pepper
  (optional)

In a large bowl, mix first three ingredients; put in a loaf or springform pan. Bake at 325 degrees for 50 minutes. Spread softened cream cheese on top. For added color and flavor, garnish with cilantro and chopped red, yellow, and green bell peppers. Slice and serve with pita bread or crackers, or with an egg dish.

PEKING PECANS

6 tbsp. butter or margarine
4 cups pecan halves
2 tbsp. soy sauce
Salt and pepper to taste

Preheat oven to 300 degrees. Melt butter or margarine. Stir and coat the pecan halves thoroughly.

Spread nuts on cookie sheet and roast for 30 minutes. Be careful not to burn. Stir once or twice. Cool two minutes. Toss with soy sauce, salt, and pepper to taste. Serve at room temperature or slightly warm. Keep in refrigerator. Can be frozen up to three months.

Nalani W. Morris
Sierra Vista, Arizona

PHEASANT STRIPS

Pheasant breasts, cut into strips
Buttermilk
Buttermilk pancake mix
Soda crackers, crushed
Sweet and sour sauce

Cut pheasant breasts into pieces approximately the same size and thickness as chicken strips. Dip breast strips into buttermilk and then into a dry mixture of equal parts buttermilk pancake mix and finely crushed soda crackers. Press dry mixture firmly onto strips. Arrange on a baking sheet and separate layers with waxed paper. Freeze at least 1 hour (keeps well up to 2 weeks in freezer if you want to make a bunch ahead of time for a crowd). Deep fry in $1/2$ inch hot oil, drain well, and serve with sweet and sour sauce.

Robert and Michele Sandness
LaMoure, North Dakota

PORTUGUESE SOUP

**1 lb. dried beans: red
kidney, pinto, navy,
blackeye, garbanzo,
or any combination**

2 large onions, chopped

2 or 3 meaty ham hocks

**2 or 3 ham slices or
small ham, cubed**

Salt to taste

2 stalks celery, sliced

2 carrots, sliced

2 potatoes, diced

**1 small cabbage,
shredded**

**1 sliced Portuguese,
Linguese, or Polish
sausage**

**1 large can tomato
sauce (15 oz.)**

**3 tomatoes, peeled and
chopped, or 1 lb. can
tomatoes**

Garlic puree, to taste

Pour 2 quarts boiling water over
washed beans and let soak about an
hour. Then add onions, ham, ham
hocks, and salt. Simmer 2-3 hours
until beans are tender.

Add remaining ingredients and
simmer until vegetables are cooked—
about 1 hour. Serve with your favorite
bread or rolls. Serves 6-8.

Nalani W. Morris
Sierra Vista, Arizona

Homemade Chicken Soup

4-5 carrots, rough chopped
2 large onions, rough chopped
2-3 stalks celery with tops, rough chopped
4 cups chicken broth
Water
4-5 chicken bouillon cubes
5 tbsp. butter or margarine
1 bay leaf
2-3 cups uncooked pasta (macaroni, egg noodles, etc.)
1 whole chicken (optional)

In a food processor or blender, liquify carrots, onions, and celery. Pour mixture into 8-qt. pot, add chicken broth, then add enough water to fill ³/₄ full. Bring to a boil and simmer for 5 minutes. Add the chicken bouillon cubes, butter or margarine, and bay leaf; simmer for 5 minutes. Add pasta noodles and bring to boil, cook until pasta is done.

NOTE: If you want to add chicken meat, either boil (and save broth) or bake a whole chicken. Pick meat off and add to soup before adding pasta noodles. Serves 8-10.

Sara A. Clark
Farmington, Connecticut

KRISTEN'S FAVORITE BURGER SOUP

2 lbs. wild game burger
Oil
1 onion, chopped
1 parsnip, sliced
3 potatoes, cubed
3 medium carrots, sliced
**¹/₂ rutabaga, peeled and
  cubed**
**1 can whole tomatoes
  (18 oz.)**
3 beef bouillon cubes
3 cups water
**¹/₂ head cabbage, cut in
  chunks**
1 bay leaf
¹/₂ tsp. dried oregano
1 tsp. salt or to taste
¹/₂ tsp. pepper

Brown meat and onions in small amount of oil. Add the rest of ingredients and simmer 1-2 hours. Serves 6.

Kristen Ward
Missoula, Montana

Elk Meatball Soup

1½ lbs. ground elk
½ cup seasoned bread crumbs
1 egg
6 cups water
3 beef bouillon cubes or 3 tsp. beef flavored instant bouillon
1 cup carrots, sliced
1 cup zucchini, sliced in 1-inch chunks
1 cup onions, coarsely chopped
1 cup celery, coarsely chopped
½ cup red bell pepper, coarsely chopped
⅓ cup rice
1 tsp. salt
⅛ tsp. pepper
2 bay leaves
¼ cup ketchup
28 oz. Italian stewed tomatoes, undrained, cut up
8 oz. tomato puree

Heat oven to 400 degrees. Line a cookie sheet with foil and coat with non-stick spray. Set aside. In a medium bowl, combine ground elk, bread crumbs, and egg. Mix well. Shape into 1-inch balls and place on cookie sheet ½ inch apart. Bake for 10 minutes.

Remove meatballs and set aside. Put remaining ingredients in 5-quart Dutch oven. Add meatballs. Bring to a boil. Reduce heat; cover and simmer 1 hour or until vegetables and rice are tender. Sprinkle soup with parmesan cheese and serve with lots of crusty French bread. Serves 12.

Luci Friday
Sacramento, California

TACO SOUP

1 lb. ground beef
1 medium onion,
  chopped
1.4 oz. dry taco mix
15 oz. stewed, ready-
  cut tomatoes
15 oz. red kidney beans,
  drained
1 can corn, drained
  (16-17 oz.)
1 can beef broth
  (10½ oz.)
3 cups water
Tortilla chips
8 oz. sour cream
1 lb. yellow cheese,
  grated

Brown beef. Add onion and cook until tender. Drain fat. Add taco mix and follow package instructions. In large kettle combine all other ingredients (except cheese, sour cream, and tortilla chips). Add beef mixture and let simmer for 30 minutes. To serve, divide chips between 6-8 soup bowls and add soup, cheese, and sour cream to each bowl. Serves 6-8.

Cathy Strasdin
Fallon, Nevada

CRAB OR SHRIMP BISQUE

¾ lb. crab meat or
  shrimp, cleaned and
  ready to cook
6 tbsp. butter
⅓ cup onions, diced
4-5 tbsp. flour
1 tsp. paprika
1 cup half-and-half
2 cups milk
½ tsp. salt
⅛ tsp. pepper

Melt butter in large saucepan over low heat. Add onions and sauté about 10 minutes. Add flour and stir constantly until a thick paste is formed. Add half-and-half and milk a little at a time, stirring until well blended and thickened. Add crab or shrimp, salt, pepper, and paprika. Continue cooking for about 15 minutes over low heat. May be made thicker by adding cornstarch mixed with small amount of water. Serves 3-4.

Jann Weber

BREADS

CHEESE BREAD TOPPING

1 lb. soft margarine
¹/₂ lb. sharp cheddar
   cheese, grated
¹/₄ lb. grated Romano
   cheese
1 tsp. Worcestershire
   sauce
¹/₄ tsp. garlic powder
¹/₂ tsp. paprika

Blend ingredients in mixer until light and fluffy. Spread on hard rolls, French bread, or English muffins, and put under broiler.

Patty Bogh
McMinnville, Oregon

ITALIAN SEASONED BREAD

Sourdough bread
Margarine
Italian seasoning

Slice sourdough bread in 1-inch slices; spread margarine on one side. Sprinkle with Italian seasoning and broil until slightly browned.

Sam Curtis
Wartburg, Tennessee

MUSTARD BRIE BREAD

French bread
Butter, softened
Dijon mustard
Brie cheese

Slice French bread; spread with softened butter, spread with small amount Dijon mustard. Put small chunks of brie cheese on top. Broil until hot and bubbly.

Linda Ward
Missoula, Montana

CARAMEL ROLL TOPPING

8 tbsp. butter (I stick)
2 tbsp. light corn syrup
I cup brown sugar,
** packed**
I tsp. vanilla
¹/₂ cup chopped walnuts

Melt butter over medium heat. Add brown sugar and syrup. Stir well, bring just to boiling point, remove from heat. Add vanilla and walnuts. Pour over bottom of pie pans and lay unbaked rolls over caramel. When baked, remove rolls quickly before caramel hardens.

Maria Mansur
Gillette, Wyoming

PARMESAN BREAD

Sourdough bread
Butter
Parmesan cheese

Slice sourdough bread in 1-inch slices. Spread butter thinly on one side of bread. Sprinkle freshly grated Parmesan cheese on top and broil until cheese melts.

Sam Curtis
Wartburg, Tennessee

Biscuits

2 cups flour
$^1/_2$ tsp. salt
4 tsp. baking powder
$^1/_2$ tsp. cream of tartar
2 tsp. sugar
$^1/_2$ cup shortening
$^2/_3$ cup milk

Sift flour, salt, baking powder, cream of tartar, and sugar together. Cut in shortening until mixture resembles coarse crumbs. Add milk all at once and stir just until dough follows fork around bowl. Roll out $^1/_2$-inch thick and cut into biscuits. Bake at 450 degrees for 10-12 minutes on ungreased cookie sheet. Makes about 2 dozen.

Ann Porter
Pleasant Hill, Missouri

Sheepherder Bread

3 cups warm water
8 tbsp. butter (1 stick)
1 cup sugar
2 pkgs. yeast
8 cups flour

Mix first four ingredients together. Let stand for 15 minutes, covered. Mix in flour one cup at a time. Knead (with hands) on floured board until mixed well. Put in large pan, cover and let rise. Punch down. Cover and let rise again. Punch down and place into pans for bread or make dinner rolls. Cover and let rise again until double. Bake in a 375-degree oven approximately 30 minutes, until brown. Makes 2 loaves.

Steven Bowen
Huson, Montana

Zucchini Bread

3 eggs
2 cups sugar
3 tsp. vanilla
1 cup oil
3 tsp. cinnamon
3 cups flour
1/4 tsp. baking powder
1 tsp. salt
1 tsp. soda
1 cup nuts
1 cup chocolate chips
2 cups zucchini, grated

Mix first four ingredients together, add dry ingredients and mix well. Stir in zucchini, nuts, and chocolate chips. Turn into two greased and floured 9 x 5-inch loaf pans. Bake at 350 degrees for 1 hour. Serves 16.

Cheryl Hall
West Linn, Oregon

Bread Rolls

1 1/2 cups water
1/2 cup milk
3 tbsp. butter
1 pkg. yeast
5 cups white flour
1 cup cracked wheat
3 tbsp. sugar
2 1/2 tsp. salt

Combine water, milk, and butter, heating until butter melts. Cool to 120-130 degrees, add yeast, stir well. Let stand 5 minutes to proof yeast. Add 2 cups flour, sugar, and salt, beating well. Stir in one more cup of flour, then add cup of cracked wheat. Add enough flour to knead. Knead on floured board for 10 minutes. Put in greased bowl; cover and let rise until double; punch down; divide into greased muffin tins for rolls. Cover and let rise. Bake at 375 degrees for about 15 minutes. Makes about 3 dozen.

Belinda M. Stockton
Orofino, Idaho

Kansas Dill Rolls

2 pkgs. dry yeast
¹/₂ cup warm water
   (110-115 degrees)
1¹/₂ cups lukewarm milk
¹/₂ cup sugar
2 tsp. salt
2 eggs
¹/₂ cup soft shortening
2 tbsp. fresh dill or
   2 tsp. dry dill
1 tsp. onion powder
7-7¹/₂ cups flour

Dissolve yeast in warm water. Let stand 5 minutes to proof yeast. Add milk, sugar, salt, eggs, shortening, seasonings, and part of flour. Mix well. Add enough additional flour to make soft dough. Knead on floured board until smooth and elastic. Place in greased bowl; cover and let rise until double. Punch down; cover and allow to rise again. Shape into rolls and place on greased sheet. Cover and let rise. Bake at 400 degrees for 12-15 minutes. Makes about 4 dozen.

Ann Porter
Pleasant Hill, Missouri

SPEEDY ROLL DOUGH (SWEET ROLLS)

2 cups hot water
²/₃ cup powdered milk
¹/₂ cup sugar
2 cakes compressed
 yeast
6 cups flour
1¹/₂ tsp. salt
1 tsp. vanilla
2 eggs
¹/₄ cup liquid shortening
1 tsp. nutmeg
Softened butter
Brown sugar
Chopped nuts

Mix first two ingredients, add sugar and yeast, and let sit 5 minutes. Mix ¹/₂ of the flour into the hot water and yeast mix. Mix in salt, vanilla, eggs, liquid shortening, and nutmeg. Beat in remaining flour until stiff. Turn out on floured surface and knead. Put back in large bowl, cover and let rise in warm place until doubled. When it has risen, divide dough into two portions and roll each into ¹/₂-inch thick rectangle. Spread soft butter on and sprinkle with brown sugar and nuts. Roll up lengthwise. Cut in ¹/₂-inch sections with a piece of thread. Bring thread up under roll and cut with back and forth motion. Lay rolls flat in pan with edges barely touching. Cover and let rise again in warm place. Bake in oven at 350 degrees for approximately 20 minutes or until golden brown. Makes about 3 dozen.

Maria Mansur
Gillette, Wyoming

BUTTERSCOTCH ROLLS

Frozen bread dough
1 pkg. butterscotch
   pudding (not instant)
   (3.5 oz.)
8 tbsp. margarine
   (1 stick)
1/2 cup brown sugar
Cinnamon

Thaw dough and form into golf ball-sized balls. Sprinkle each bread ball with cinnamon. Place in well-greased tube pan. Sprinkle with dry pudding. Melt margarine and add brown sugar. Pour over rolls. Cover with foil and place in refrigerator overnight. Next morning, bake at 375 degrees for 30-35 minutes. Leave foil on during baking. Serves 10.

Yvonne Decker
Libby, Montana

PARSLEY DUMPLINGS

2 cups flour
1 tbsp. baking powder
1/2 tsp. salt
1/2 tsp. dried thyme
1/2 tsp. nutmeg
3/4 cup finely chopped
   fresh parsley
1 tbsp. butter or
   margarine
3 egg yolks
3/4 cup cold milk

Sift together the flour, baking powder, salt, thyme, and nutmeg. Add parsley. Cut in butter until mixture resembles corn meal. Beat egg yolks into milk; add liquid to flour mixture. Mix quickly until ingredients are moistened, but do not beat. Drop dough by tablespoons into simmering soup or stew. Cover pot tightly and cook for 12 minutes without removing the cover. Serves 4-6.

Paulette Nelson
Mesa, Arizona

WAGNER'S FRIED BREAD

3 cups flour
2 tbsp. baking powder
1 tbsp. sugar
1 tsp. salt
1 tbsp. lard or
   shortening
2 cups cold water
Oil

Mix dry ingredients; cut in shortening. Add enough water to make thick dough and knead well. Heat oil in deep-fryer at 350 degrees. Break off handfuls of dough and fry until golden brown. Drain and serve warm with butter or jam. Serves 8-10.

Bernis Wagner
Roseburg, Oregon

SOUTHWEST CORN BREAD

2 large eggs
$^1/_4$ cup granulated sugar
1 cup plain yogurt
1 cup flour
1 cup yellow cornmeal
2 tsp. baking powder
1 tsp. baking soda
$^1/_2$ cup whole kernel
   canned corn
1 can chopped mild
   green chilies, drained
   (4.5 oz.)
4 tbsp. margarine,
   melted
1 tbsp. finely chopped
   red bell pepper

Beat eggs and sugar together in large bowl. Stir in yogurt. Combine flour, cornmeal, baking powder, and baking soda in medium bowl. Blend into the yogurt mixture. Add corn, chilies, and butter. Mix well. Spoon into greased 9 x 9-inch baking dish and sprinkle the pepper pieces evenly on top. Bake in a 425-degree oven until golden, 15-20 minutes. Serve warm. Serves 8.

Donna Saasen
Tacoma, Washington

PARTY CORN BREAD

2 cans whole kernel corn, undrained (16 oz. each)
1 can creamed corn (16 oz.)
2 boxes Jiffy corn muffin mix (8¹/₂ oz.)
¹/₂ lb. butter, melted
2 eggs, beaten
1 carton sour cream (16 oz.)

Mix ingredients well and put in a greased 9 x 13-inch pan. Bake at 350 degrees for 45-50 minutes or until a knife comes out clean. Serves 12-15.

Bonnie Swanson
Butte, Montana

Sourdough Starter

2 cups flour
2 cups warm water
¼ cup granulated sugar
1 envelope yeast

Mix flour, water, sugar, and yeast together in plastic or glass container and let stand overnight, loosely covered, in a warm place. The next day, refrigerate, loosely covered. Stir every day.

On the fifth day, add to the mixture: 1 cup flour, 1 cup milk, and ½ cup sugar. Stir well and return to the refrigerator. Continue stirring daily.

On the tenth day, you can use the starter. Remove 1 cup and set aside. Return 1 cup of the starter to the empty crock. To it add 1 cup flour, 1 cup milk, and ½ cup sugar. Repeat additions on the fifth day. Remember to stir each day.

On the tenth day, you will be ready to bake again, or add 1 tsp. sugar to the starter and repeat every tenth day until you are ready to bake. (But don't wait too long, or you won't be able to get anything else in the refrigerator.)

When you give a friend 1 cup of the starter, have him or her add 1 cup flour, 1 cup milk, ½ cup sugar, and stir each day. On the fifth day the friend will be able to use it, which cuts off 5 days from the start-up time. Recipes on the next 4 pages will get the starter out of the refrigerator and put it to work.

Les Roberts
Eugene, Oregon

ORANGE CINNAMON SOURDOUGH ROLLS

2 cups self-rising flour
³/₄ cup sourdough starter
²/₃ cup buttermilk
3 tbsp. melted butter
¹/₂ cup granulated sugar
1 tbsp. orange peel,
  chopped fine
2 tsp. ground cinnamon
1 tbsp. melted butter

ICING:
1 cup powdered sugar
2 tbsp. milk
¹/₃ tsp. vanilla

Combine the flour, starter, and buttermilk. Knead 15 times on a floured board. Roll and shape into a 12-inch square. Brush dough with the 3 tbsp. melted butter. Combine sugar, orange peel, and cinnamon. Sprinkle over dough. Roll dough in jellyroll fashion. Seal edges.

Cut roll into twelve 1-inch slices. Place slices in a greased 9-inch square pan. Brush with the remaining 1 tbsp. butter and bake in a 375-degree oven 20-25 minutes. Turn out on rack and drizzle with icing. For icing, combine powdered sugar, milk, and vanilla until well blended.

Les Roberts
Eugene, Oregon

SOURDOUGH COFFEE CAKE

2 cups sourdough starter
2 eggs
2 cups flour
$^{1}/_{2}$ tsp. baking soda
2 tbsp. baking powder
1 $^{1}/_{2}$ tsp. ground cinnamon
1 cup granulated sugar
$^{2}/_{3}$ cup vegetable oil
$^{1}/_{2}$ tsp. salt
1-2 cups any dried,
     frozen, fresh, or
     drained canned fruit

CINNAMON TOPPING:
1 cup brown sugar
1 tbsp. flour
$^{1}/_{2}$ tsp. ground cinnamon
$^{1}/_{4}$ cup butter

BROWN SUGAR GLAZE:
3 tbsp. butter
1 cup brown sugar
$^{1}/_{4}$ cup milk

Stir together starter, eggs, flour, baking soda, baking powder, cinnamon, sugar, oil, salt, and fruit. Spread batter in greased 9 x 13-inch pan.

To prepare the topping, cream together brown sugar, flour, cinnamon, and butter. Sprinkle topping over the batter in the pan. Bake in a 350-degree oven for 45 minutes. While cake is baking, prepare glaze. Simmer butter, brown sugar, and milk together for 5 minutes. Pour glaze over hot coffee cake as soon as it is removed from the oven. Serves 6-8.

Les Roberts
Eugene, Oregon

SOURDOUGH ROLLS

¹/₂ cup sugar
4 cups flour
2 cups water
**1 cup sourdough starter,
    room temperature**

Mix all ingredients. Mixing bowl should be fairly large, because if it is warm in the kitchen, the starter will be tremendously active.

In the morning for noontime rolls, or about noon for evening rolls, put dough on a floured board, using only enough flour so it can be handled and shaped easily. When mixed and kneaded, it can be made into two loaves or 16 orange-sized rolls, or anything in between. Place in greased pan, iron skillet, or better still, glass baking dish. Turn rolls over so all sides are greased and let rise until double in bulk—about 2¹/₂ hours in really warm weather. Place in cold oven and bake at 325 degrees for 1 hour. This is a salt-free recipe, but salt to taste may be added before shaping into rolls. Remember that salt will kill some of the action if it is added too soon.

Les Roberts
Eugene, Oregon

Sourdough Pancakes

Sourdough starter
Flour as needed
Milk as needed
Baking soda (optional)

The starter itself may be used for pancakes, adding only enough flour or milk for the proper consistency (buttermilk is ideal). If too sour for taste, a pinch or more of baking soda will tone it down.

Les Roberts
Eugene, Oregon

SALADS AND
VEGETABLES

Exotic Turkey Salad

8 cups cooked turkey,
  coarsely cut
1 can water chestnuts,
  sliced (8 oz.)
2 lbs. seedless grapes
2 cups sliced celery
1 1/2 cups toasted slivered
  almonds
1 can pineapple chunks
  (8 oz.)

DRESSING:
3 cups mayonnaise
1 tbsp. each curry and
  lemon juice
2 tbsp. soy sauce

Mix together turkey, water chestnuts, grapes, celery, almonds, and pineapple. Combine dressing ingredients. Add to turkey mixture. Chill at least 1 hour. Serves 8-10.

Mollie Fouts
Puyallup, Washington

Broccoli Salad

2 large bunches broccoli
1 medium onion,
  chopped
1 can water chestnuts
  (8 oz.)
12 strips cooked bacon,
  crumbled
1 1/2 cups sunflower seeds,
  salted or unsalted

DRESSING:
1 cup Miracle Whip
1/2 cup sugar
2 tbsp. vinegar

Discard woody part of broccoli stem. Peel remaining stem and chop it and broccoli heads. Combine broccoli, onion, and water chestnuts. Mix together dressing ingredients. Add dressing to salad 2 hours before serving and toss. Refrigerate. Just before serving, drain off excess dressing and add bacon and sunflower seeds. Serves 12 or more.

Salle Rice
Butte, Montana

Mexican Salad Buffet

MEAT SAUCE:

6 lbs. ground elk, deer, or beef

4 large onions, finely chopped

6 cans hot chili beans (15 oz. each)

6 cans enchilada hot sauce (10 oz. each)

Salt to taste

BUFFET INGREDIENTS:

4 bags coarsely broken corn chips

Meat sauce

4 heads chopped iceberg lettuce, mixed with an 8 oz. bottle of Italian salad dressing

6 bunches green onions, chopped

10-12 tomatoes, peeled and chopped

2 lbs. grated cheddar cheese

4 to 6 mashed avocados, mixed with lemon juice

Sour cream

Stir and cook meat in large, heavy kettle until it loses its redness. Add the onions and continue to cook until transparent. Add beans and enchilada sauce, rinsing each can with a little water and adding to mixture. Bring to boil, then simmer. Add a couple teaspoons of salt (more if necessary) and cover. The cooking should be long and slow, 6-8 hours or overnight in a tightly covered roasting pan at 200 degrees. Refrigerate and skim off fat. For the dinner, place the buffet ingredients in separate bowls. The guests can add to their plates in any order they please.

All ingredients can be chopped ahead except tomatoes and avocados. Don't add the Italian salad dressing to lettuce until just before serving. Serves 20-25.

Nalani W. Morris
Sierra Vista, Arizona

Linda's Spicy Black Bean Salad

1½ cups dried black
   beans or black-eyed
   peas
1 small green bell
   pepper, chopped
1 small carrot, coarsely
   grated
1 tbsp. chopped red
   onion
4 tbsp. lime juice
½ tsp. dried cumin
   and/or ¼ tsp. red
   pepper flakes
2 tbsp. oil
1 clove garlic, minced
¼ tsp. ground pepper
¼ tsp. salt (optional)
Chopped fresh cilantro
   to taste

Soak beans in water to cover overnight. Rinse, add fresh water, and cook 45 minutes or until tender. Drain. Add vegetables to cooked black beans. In another bowl, mix remaining ingredients and pour over bean mixture. Let stand. Serve at room temperature. Serves 4-6.

Linda Ward
Missoula, Montana

FOUR BEAN SALAD

1 can green beans
  (16 oz.)
1 can wax beans (16 oz.)
1 can kidney beans
  (16 oz.)
1 can garbanzo beans
  (15 oz.)
1/2 cup chopped celery
1/2 medium onion, sliced
  into rings
1 bottle Italian dressing
  (8 oz.)
1 tbsp. sugar

Drain all the beans. Combine all four beans, celery, and onion rings in a bowl, and season with dressing and sugar. Lightly toss so all ingredients are coated. Cover and refrigerate for several hours or overnight. Serves 12 or more.

Sharon Robertson
Kansas City, Kansas

OVERNIGHT SALAD

1/2 head lettuce,
  shredded
1 head cauliflower
2 cups mayonnaise
12 oz. bacon, fried crisp
  and crumbled
1/2 cup Parmesan cheese
1/4 cup sugar

Break cauliflower into flowerets; do not use stems in salad. Using an attractive glass serving bowl, alternate layers of ingredients. Try to use each ingredient twice. Cover and let set overnight in refrigerator. Serves 8.

Yvonne Decker
Libby, Montana

Huckleberry Salad

1 pkg. raspberry or
  other red Jell-O
  (6 oz.)
2 cups boiling water
2 cups frozen or fresh
  huckleberries
1 can crushed pineapple
  (16 oz.)

Mix Jell-O and boiling water. Cool in refrigerator. Fold in berries and pineapple before it jells. Put in gelatin mold. Serves 8-10.

Yvonne Decker
Libby, Montana

Strawberry Whip Salad

1 pkg. frozen
  strawberries, thawed
  (10 oz.)
1 cup pecans, chopped
1 pkg. strawberry gelatin
  (6 oz.)
1 pt. whipping cream,
  whipped

Combine strawberries with their juice, pecans, and dry gelatin in bowl; mix well. Fold in whipped cream. Pour into 8-inch square pan. Chill until firm. Cut into squares. Serves 8.

Frog Eye Salad (acini de pepe salad)

³/₄ cup sugar

I tbsp. flour

¹/₂ tsp. salt

²/₃ cup pineapple juice

I egg, beaten

I tsp. lemon juice

I cup acini de pepe (pasta)

2 cans mandarin oranges, drained (11 oz. each)

I can chunk pineapple, drained (20 oz.)

I can crushed pineapple, drained (20 oz.)

I carton Cool Whip (8 oz.)

I cup miniature marshmallows

In small saucepan, mix sugar, flour, and salt. Stir in pineapple juice and egg. Cook over moderate heat, stirring constantly until thickened. Add lemon juice. Set aside and cool.

Cook *acini de pepe* pasta according to package directions. Drain pasta. Combine cooked mixture with pasta. Cover and place in refrigerator until chilled (about 4 hours or overnight). Add remaining ingredients. Stir lightly. Chill at least 1 hour before serving. Serves 8-10.

Sharon Kilmer
Arlington, Washington

BROCCOLI MARINADE

¹/₂ cup cider vinegar
¹/₂ cup sugar
¹/₂ tsp. celery seed
1 tsp. minced onion
1 cup vegetable oil
1 tsp. salt
2 bunches broccoli

Mix or shake all ingredients, except broccoli, together. Cut off tough part of broccoli stem. Peel and chop rest of stem. Break broccoli tops into flowerets. Add broccoli to marinade mixture; mix or shake until coated with marinade. Put in refrigerator, covered, for 2-3 hours. Drain before serving. Serves 12.

Sara A. Clark
Farmington, Connecticut

CROCK SALAD

1 large head cabbage
2 large carrots, peeled
1 green pepper
¹/₂ cup onion, chopped
3 stalks celery
1 tbsp. salt

DRESSING:
2 cups sugar
2 cups vinegar
2 tbsp. celery seed
2 tbsp. white mustard
  seed

Chop cabbage, carrots, celery, and green pepper. Put into big crock with onion. Cover with water and stir in 1 tbsp. salt. Let stand overnight. Make dressing by combining dressing ingredients in a sauce pan, bring to a boil, and let cool. Drain salt water from vegetables, pour dressing over. Put in covered container and store in a cool place until ready to serve. Serves 12.

Ann Porter
Pleasant Hill, Missouri

Italian Salad with Parmesan Dressing

Salad Ingredients:

I small head romaine
   lettuce, torn
¹/₂ head iceberg lettuce,
   torn (or use assorted
   other greens)
¹/₄ lb. Italian salami,
   sliced, then cut into
   strips
¹/₄ lb. mozzarella,
   coarsely shredded
I cup garbanzo beans,
   rinsed and drained
I-2 tomatoes cut in
   small wedges
I¹/₂ cup fresh
   mushrooms, sliced

Dressing:

5 tbsp. vegetable oil
2 tbsp. white wine
   vinegar
2 tbsp. dry mustard
I tsp. salt
¹/₂ tsp. pepper
¹/₂ cup grated Parmesan
   cheese

Combine salad ingredients in bowl. Combine dressing ingredients and pour over salad. Toss to coat. Serves 12.

Linda Ward
Missoula, Montana

Dirty Mashed Potatoes

**3 large Idaho baking
   potatoes**
1 tsp. garlic salt
4 tbsp. margarine
2 tbsp. sour cream
Milk
Salt and pepper to taste

Wash and scrub potatoes, leaving peel on. Cut into boiling pieces as you would regular mashed potatoes. Boil approximately 20 minutes or until tender. Drain and mash until slightly chunky. Add margarine, sour cream, garlic salt, and salt and pepper to taste. Add milk as needed to create right consistency. Leave slightly chunky. Serves 4.

VARIATION: Add 4 oz. grated cheddar cheese and warm over low heat until cheese melts.

Sam Curtis
Wartburg, Tennessee

Party Potatoes

**2 lbs. frozen hash
   browns, partially
   thawed**
1 cup finely diced onions
**1 can cream of chicken
   soup (10½ oz.)**
¼ cup melted margarine
**1 carton sour cream
   (16 oz.)**
**8 oz. grated cheddar
   cheese**
**1 cup crushed potato
   chips**
Salt and pepper

Mix onions, soup, margarine, sour cream, salt and pepper together. Add to partially thawed hash browns. Put in 9 x 13-inch casserole dish. Sprinkle with cheese and potato chips. Bake at 375 degrees for 1 hour. Serves 12.

Sharon Robertson
Kansas City, Kansas

PARMESAN RED POTATOES

8 red potatoes (about
   2 per person)
^{1}/$_2$ cup olive oil
^{1}/$_2$ cup Parmesan cheese
4 tbsp. fresh tarragon,
   chopped, or 2 tbsp.
   dried

Cut tennis-ball-sized red potatoes into eighths and place on cookie sheet. Dribble olive oil over the potatoes and bake at 350 degrees for 20 minutes. Remove from oven and sprinkle Parmesan cheese and tarragon (rosemary also works great if having red meat) over the potatoes. Put back in the oven for 15 minutes or until done. Serves 4-8.

James E. Pinch
Bellevue, Washington

STUFFED POTATOES

1 lb. elk burger
1 egg
^{1}/$_2$ cup chopped onion
Salt and pepper to taste
4 baking potatoes
2 tbsp. butter
^{1}/$_2$ cup water
White sauce
Grated Swiss cheese

Mix burger, egg, onions, salt, and pepper. Slice off the top third lengthwise of each potato. With a spoon, hollow out, leaving more than ^{1}/$_4$-inch of potato on bottom and sides. Put burger mixture into hollowed-out cavity. Replace tops. Place in a two-quart pan. Dot with butter. Put water in bottom of pan. Cover. Bake at 375 degrees for 60 minutes. Serve with white sauce or top with white sauce, sprinkle with grated Swiss cheese, and broil until golden brown. Serves 4.

Yvonne Decker
Libby, Montana

GINGER CARROTS

8 large carrots, peeled
¹/₂ tsp. salt
¹/₂ cup honey
4 tbsp. sugar
4 tbsp. margarine
I tsp. grated lemon rind
¹/₄ tsp. powdered ginger

Cut carrots into your favorite shape and cook in small amount of salted water, covered, for 10 minutes. Drain and add honey, sugar, and margarine. Cook uncovered, stirring occasionally, until carrots are tender and glazed. Stir in lemon rind and ginger. Serve immediately. Serves 8-12.

Miriam L. Jones
Eugene, Oregon

RED CABBAGE WITH APPLE

I ¹/₂-2 lbs. red cabbage,
** shredded**
¹/₂ cup water
2 medium apples, pared,
** cored, sliced**
2 tbsp. melted butter or
** margarine**
¹/₄ cup vinegar
I ¹/₂ tsp. flour
¹/₄ cup brown sugar,
** packed**
I tbsp. Mrs. Dash

Put shredded cabbage in pan with water; bring to boil and cook, covered, for 10 minutes. Add apples; cook covered for 10 minutes until tender. Combine butter, vinegar, flour, sugar, Mrs. Dash; add to cabbage-apple mixture. Serves 4-6.

Margaret C. Robinson
Pelham, New Hampshire

SCRUMPTIOUS KRAUT DISH

2 cups sauerkraut,
   drained
2 cups canned tomatoes,
   drained
1 small onion, chopped
   (or 2 tbsp. instant)
$^1/_3$ cup sugar
4 cooked bacon strips,
   crumbled

Mix all ingredients together. Microwave on high for 10 minutes or bake at 350 degrees for 45 minutes or until hot. Serves 4-8.

Salle Rice
Butte, Montana

DUTCH OVEN CABBAGE

1 head cabbage
Bacon
1 onion, chopped
1 cup water (or beer)
Honey
Chili powder, or canned
   green chilies

To start, slice up bacon into pieces and fry in a hot dutch oven. When half done, add one chopped onion. When the onion is tender but not brown, add one cup of water or an equal amount of beer. Now add one head of cabbage sliced into thin wedges or chopped. Depending on the crowd, you might want 2 heads of cabbage. Put on the lid and keep at a slow boil. Check to keep enough liquid. I add chili power and green chilies. I always add honey. You can tell when it is done by tasting. Serves 6-8.

Jack Lutch
Wickenburg, Arizona

Snow Peas and Carrots

2 tbsp. butter
¹/₄ lb. fresh snow peas
2 large carrots
I tbsp. sugar
Salt and pepper to taste

String snowpeas. Peel and cut carrots into thin strips about 2 inches long. Sauté carrots and snow peas in butter over medium heat until tender. Add sugar and salt and pepper to taste and sauté 30 seconds longer. Serves 2-4.

Sam Curtis
Wartburg, Tennessee

Pickled Beets

4 quart jars
4 cups sugar
4 cups vinegar
4 cups water
Beets

Pull beets when they are the size of a quarter (little beets are the best). Clean, and cook until tender. Remove stems. Pack in sterile jars. Bring to a boil equal parts of sugar, vinegar, and water. Let boil a few minutes and then add boiling liquid to cover beets in jars. Add 2-3 whole cloves, ¹/₂ stick cinnamon, and a pinch of allspice per jar. Seal jars.

Ann Porter
Pleasant Hill, Missouri

Fresh Cucumber Pickles

7 cups sliced cucumbers
2 cups sliced onions
I cup sliced green
  pepper
2 tbsp. coarse salt
I tsp. celery seed
I cup cider vinegar
2 cups sugar

Mix vegetables, salt, and celery seed. Dissolve sugar in vinegar. Pour over vegetables and mix well. The mixture may seem to need more liquid, but after a night in the refrigerator, there will be plenty. Put into pint jars, cover, and keep refrigerated. Keeps in the refrigerator for weeks. Makes 1½ quarts.

Kay Stevenson
and Ann Porter
Pleasant Hill, Missouri

Plain Dill Pickles

8 small cucumbers,
  2-4 inches—enough to
  fill 4 quart jars
Fresh dill
2 qts. water
4 cups vinegar
I cup salt

Wash cucumbers and pack them in sterilized jars with 3-5 sprigs of dill in each jar. Bring to a boil water, vinegar, and salt. Let boil a few minutes and then pour over the cucumbers to cover. Seal jars.

Ann Porter
Pleasant Hill, Missouri

BEANS, RICE, AND PASTA

Calico Beans

¹/₂ lb. bacon, chopped
1 can each of pork and
  beans, kidney beans,
  and lima beans
  (21 oz. each)
1 lb. ground venison
1 cup chopped onion
1 garlic clove, chopped
¹/₂ cup ketchup
¹/₄ cup brown sugar
¹/₄ cup white sugar
1 tsp. prepared mustard
1 tsp. salt
2 tsp. vinegar
1 tbsp. Liquid Smoke

Cook bacon. Remove with slotted spoon to drain. Add venison, garlic, and onion to bacon grease. Cook until onion is tender. Drain off excess grease. Drain cans of beans and place in oven-proof casserole. Add meat mixture and remaining ingredients. Mix. Bake at 350 degrees for 40 minutes. Serves 12-15.

Sharon Robertson
Kansas City, Kansas

ARLENE'S BEANS

1 large can baked beans
   (28 oz.)
1 lb. hamburger
2 tbsp. brown sugar
2 tbsp. Worcestershire
   sauce
1/2 medium onion,
   chopped
1 small can mushrooms
   (7 oz.)
1 small can tomato
   sauce (8 oz.)

Brown burger and onions. Add all other ingredients and heat at 350 degrees for 1 hour. Serves 8.

Arlene Selchert
Chehalis, Washington

WILD RICE CASSEROLE

4 tbsp. margarine or
   butter
1 box long grain wild
   rice w/seasonings
   (6 oz.)
1/2 cup slivered almonds
2 tbsp. chopped green
   onions
2 cans mushrooms,
   drained (4 oz. each)
2 cans beef broth
   (10 1/2 oz. each)

Melt margarine or butter in oven-proof casserole on top of stove. Add rice w/seasonings, almonds, green onions, and mushrooms. Cook rice mixture until white rice turns cloudy. Be careful not to scorch. Add broth and heat to simmering. Cover and bake 1 hour at 350 degrees. Serves 4.

Harriet Parks
Alpine, Wyoming

ALMOND MUSHROOM CHOP SUEY

I tbsp. cooking oil
I cup onion, sliced
I cup celery, sliced
¹/₂-I cup green pepper,
   sliced
I-2 cups fresh bean
   sprouts
I-2 cups fresh
   mushrooms, sliced
I-2 tbsp. soy sauce to
   taste
Wild rice
4 tbsp. toasted almonds

Sauté onion and celery in oil until just tender (about 3 minutes). Add remaining vegetables. Cover and cook over low heat until green pepper is tender. Stir in soy sauce. Serve over cooked wild rice. Top with toasted almonds. Serves 4.

Lorna Dorey
Rocky Mountain House,
Alberta

LEMON PECAN WILD RICE

2 cups canned chicken
   broth
Rind of ¹/₂ lemon
   removed with a
   vegetable peeler and
   cut into julienne strips
   (about 1¹/₂ tbsp.)
I tbsp. fresh lemon juice
I tbsp. unsalted butter
I cup wild rice, rinsed
   and drained well
¹/₂ cup pecans, toasted
   lightly and chopped
3 tbsp. minced scallions
¹/₄ cup minced fresh
   parsley

In a heavy saucepan combine broth, half the rind, lemon juice, and butter. Bring mixture to a boil, and stir in rice. Cook the rice, covered, over low heat for 50 minutes to 1 hour, or until it is tender and has absorbed the liquid. Stir in pecans, scallions, parsley, and remaining rind. Add salt and pepper to taste. Serves 4.

Shelley Gilligan
Hillsborough, California

DJ's Green Rice

2 cups Minute Rice
1 clove garlic, diced
1 medium onion,
    chopped
2 tbsp. vegetable oil
1¹/₂-1³/₄ lb. Old English
    Cheese, grated
1 pkg. frozen chopped
    broccoli (10 oz.),
    thawed and drained
Salt to taste
1 egg
1 cup milk

Cook rice according to package directions. Drain and place in a large baking bowl or dish. Sauté garlic and onion in oil until onion is translucent. Add onion, broccoli, and cheese (save some cheese for the top) to the rice. Salt to taste. Beat together the egg and milk, then add to above mixture. Mix all ingredients well. Sprinkle remaining cheese on top. Bake at 350 degrees for 30 minutes. Serves 6-8.

Sharon Robertson
Kansas City, Kansas

ELK LASAGNA

Lasagna noodles
16 oz. mozzarella
  cheese, shredded

MEAT FILLING:
1 lb. elk burger
1 medium onion,
  chopped
1 clove garlic, chopped
1 jar spaghetti sauce
  (32 oz.)
1 cup mushrooms,
  chopped
1 can tomato paste
  (6 oz.)
1 pinch dried rosemary
1 pinch powdered cloves
1 pinch powdered
  allspice
2 tbsp. fresh parsley,
  chopped
1 tsp. sugar

CHEESE FILLING:
1 carton cottage cheese
  (16 oz.)
1/4 cup Parmesan cheese
1 tbsp. fresh parsley,
  chopped

Brown burger in large pan. Add onions and garlic and cook until onions are just tender. Add remaining meat filling ingredients and simmer 1 hour. Mix together cheese filling ingredients. Place a thin layer of meat sauce on bottom of 13 x 9-inch baking pan. Add a layer of cooked or uncooked lasagna noodles. If using uncooked noodles, add 1/2-3/4 cup more sauce. Divide meat sauce into thirds and cheese filling in half. Spread layer of meat sauce on noodles and then a layer of cheese filling. Top with 1/2 of mozzarella. Then repeat noodles, meat, cheese filling and mozzarella, ending with noodles and sauce. Spread the top with Parmesan cheese and bake in oven at 350 degrees for 1 hour. Let stand 10 minutes before serving. Serves 9-12.

Jayne Gallion
Buckley, Washington

VENISON SPAGHETTI

1 1/2 lbs. venison, elk, or
   moose burger
1 medium onion,
   chopped
5 cloves minced garlic
2 cans whole tomatoes
   (14 1/2 oz. each)
2 tbsp. olive oil
1 can tomato paste
   (6 oz.)
1/2 cup red wine
1/2 lb. hot Italian sausage
   (optional)
1 cup mushrooms, sliced
Dash of Worcestershire
   sauce
1 bay leaf
1 tsp. oregano
1/2 tsp. rosemary
1/2 tsp. basil
1/2 tsp. margarine
Salt and pepper to taste
Freshly grated Parmesan
   cheese.

In olive oil, brown burger and hot Italian sausage with onion and garlic. Drain. Add remaining ingredients (except Parmesan cheese) and simmer at least 30 minutes. Serve sauce over cooked spaghetti and top with Parmesan cheese. Serves 6-9.

Sam Curtis
Wartburg, Tennessee

QUICK VENISON SPAGHETTI

1 lb. venison, elk, or
   moose burger
1 tbsp. olive oil
2 cloves garlic, minced
1 jar spaghetti sauce
   (32 oz.)
1 can mushrooms (4 oz.)
1 tbsp. oregano, dried
Salt and pepper to taste
Freshly grated Parmesan
   cheese

In olive oil, brown burger with garlic and drain excess fat. Add spaghetti sauce, mushrooms, oregano, and salt and pepper to taste. Simmer 10 minutes. Serve on cooked spaghetti and top each portion with Parmesan cheese. Makes about 6 cups of sauce. Serves 4-6.

Sam Curtis
Wartburg, Tennessee

Italian Meatball Spaghetti

SAUCE:

1/2 large onion, chopped
3 cloves garlic, mashed
1 can sliced mushrooms
   (4 oz.)
Olive oil
1 quart whole tomatoes
1 quart tomato sauce
1 can tomato paste (6 oz.)
Up to 3 "paste" cans of
   water (do not add this
   water if using home-
   canned tomatoes or
   tomato sauce)
1 tbsp. fresh parsley,
   chopped
2 bay leaves
1 tsp. dried oregano
1 tsp. dried basil
1 tsp. sugar
2 tbsp. Parmesan cheese
Salt and pepper

MEATBALLS:

1 lb. lean ground elk burger
1 lb. sweet or hot Italian
   sausage, crumbled
1/2 large onion, finely diced
3 eggs
1 tbsp. fresh parsley,
   chopped
1/2 cup bread crumbs
Salt and pepper

Spaghetti noodles

In large kettle, sauté onions and garlic in small amount of olive oil until onions are translucent. Add remaining ingredients and cook slowly for several hours or longer.

Mix meatball ingredients together, form into 1¹/₂-inch balls, and brown thoroughly in lightly oiled frying pan. Add to spaghetti sauce mixture and allow to cook slowly with the sauce. Do not stir briskly. Cook dried spaghetti in large pan of boiling water to which a small amount of olive oil has been added to keep noodles from sticking. Use 2-3 ounces dried spaghetti per person. Serve meatballs and sauce over spaghetti. Serves 8-10.

Connie Nolin
Kalispell, Montana

FOWL

Sweet and Sour Quail

1 1/2 cups brown sugar
1/2 cup vinegar
1/2 cup water
1 tsp. dry mustard
8 or 9 quail
2 tbsp. cornstarch
1 tbsp. water

Place first 4 ingredients in a glass bowl. Microwave 1 minute on high. Place quail in a round glass dish. Pour sauce over. Partially cover. Microwave 17 minutes on high. Let stand 10 minutes. Drain the sauce off and thicken with cornstarch mixed with water. Microwave 2-3 minutes on high. Pour sauce over the quail on a serving platter. The vinegar tenderizes wild game and can be used on other birds like pheasant and duck. To cook in conventional oven, bake, covered, at 350 degrees for 1 hour. Serves 8-9.

Salle Rice
Butte, Montana

QUAIL AND RASPBERRY SAUCE

16 quail, each about
  4 oz.
2 to 3 tbsp. salad oil
¹/₃ cup sugar
¹/₂ cup raspberry vinegar
  or red wine vinegar
2 cups regular strength
  chicken broth
1¹/₂ tbsp. cornstarch
1¹/₂ tbsp. water
1 cup fresh or partially
  thawed, frozen,
  unsweetened
  raspberries
2 tbsp. brandy
2 tbsp. lemon juice
Salt and pepper

Rinse birds and pat dry; save necks and giblets for another use. Pour 2 tbsp. oil into a 10-12 inch frying pan over medium-high heat. Add birds, a few at a time (do not crowd), and brown all over, about 5 minutes per bird; add additional oil as needed. Arrange birds, breast up and slightly apart, on a rack in a 12 x 17-inch roasting pan.

Roast birds in a 400-degree oven until breasts are still red and moist in center but not wet-looking (cut into breast just above wing joint to test), 12-15 minutes. Keep warm in a 150-degree oven up to 30 minutes while making sauce. Reserve roasting juices.

Add sugar and 1 tbsp. vinegar to the frying pan. Cook over medium high heat until sugar liquefies and turns a golden caramel color, 3-5 minutes. While stirring, add remaining vinegar; simmer, stirring until caramel dissolves, about 2 minutes. Add broth and quail roasting juices; boil, uncovered, until reduced by half—about 15 minutes.

Mix cornstarch and water; stir into sauce. Stir until boiling. Add raspberries, brandy, lemon juice, and salt and pepper to taste. Pour over birds. Serves 8.

Vickie Hopp
Bend, Oregon

PHEASANT AND RICE CASSEROLE

1 pheasant, cut up
1 can cream of chicken soup (10³/₄ oz.)
1 can water or milk
1 pkg. dry onion soup mix
³/₄ cup uncooked rice (add a little wild rice for color, but be sure to partially cook the wild rice first)

Place rice in casserole dish. Arrange pheasant on top. Mix together soup, water, and onion soup mix. Pour over pheasant and rice. Bake covered 1 hour at 350 degrees. Cook an additional 30 minutes uncovered to brown. Serves 4.

Robert and Michele Sandness
LaMoure, North Dakota

PHEASANT PROVENCE

2 whole pheasant breasts
Flour
Salt and pepper
Paprika
Herbs de Provence spice
¹/₄ cup garlic-flavored oil
2 tbsp. butter
1-2 tbsp. lemon juice
Dash of vermouth or other white wine

Clean and separate halves of 2 pheasant breasts. Pound each half flat. Heat butter and oil in fry pan. Salt, pepper, and flour the breasts and sauté for about 2 minutes per side. Sprinkle paprika and *Herbs de Provence* spice on each side as the meat is cooking. Place breasts on a serving plate. Deglaze the frying pan with lemon juice and vermouth. This will make a light lemon sauce that is poured on top of the breasts before service. Serve with cooked wild rice or rice pilaf and vegetables. Serves 4.

Lyn Neel
Eugene, Oregon

BAKED PHEASANT, QUAIL, GROUSE, OR DOVE IN CREAM SAUCE

2 pheasants or 4 quail
Seasoned flour
3 tbsp. butter
1/2 lb. fresh mushrooms, sliced
1/3 cup sliced almonds
1/2 small onion, chopped
3 celery stalks, chopped
1 pint heavy cream
1 tsp. salt
1 tsp. pepper
1 cup sherry

Quarter or halve birds. Dip in seasoned flour and brown in butter. Set aside. Sauté mushrooms, almonds, onion, and celery in remaining butter. Place birds in Dutch oven and pour sautéed mixture over them. Cover and bake at 350 degrees for 1 1/2 hours. Add cream, salt, pepper, and sherry. Cover and bake an additional 30 minutes or until birds are tender. Serves 4.

Sue Gooding
Albuquerque, New Mexico

PHEASANT STROGANOFF

2 pheasants
Flour
2 tbsp. cooking oil
1 cup white wine
¹/₂ cup onion, chopped
**1 can cream of
    mushroom soup
    (10³/₄ oz.)**
1 cup sour cream
**¹/₄ lb. fresh mushrooms,
    sliced and sautéed**

Cut legs and thighs off pheasants; fillet each breast and cut them up into bite-size pieces. Lightly flour legs and thighs and brown in 1 tbsp. cooking oil. Add white wine and chopped onion. Simmer legs and thighs for about 1-2 hours, until the meat is falling off the bones. Remove, cool, and remove all meat from bones. Set aside.

Make a sauce out of the wine and onions in which the legs and thighs were simmering by adding 1 can cream of mushroom soup, 1 cup sour cream, and ¹/₄ lb. sautéed, sliced mushrooms. Add salt and pepper to taste. Lightly flour the breast pieces and saute them in 1 tbsp. oil for 3-4 minutes. Add all meat to the cream sauce. Heat and serve over cooked wild rice. Serves 6-8.

*Shelley Gilligan
Hillsborough, California*

PHEASANT IN WINE SAUCE

2 pheasants cut into
   fryer pieces
3 cloves garlic, chopped
2 tbsp. olive oil
$^1/_2$ cup white wine
1 large can tomato
   sauce (15 oz.)
2 cups water
1 large onion, chopped
8 oz. fresh mushrooms,
   sliced
$^1/_4$ tsp. salt
$^1/_4$ tsp. dried tarragon
$^1/_4$ tsp. dried marjoram
$^1/_4$ tsp. crushed pepper
   or peppercorns
$^1/_4$ tsp. dried sage
1 tbsp. parsley flakes
   or fresh parsley,
   chopped

Take two small pheasants, cut into fryer parts (skin and bone as much as possible). Sauté garlic in olive oil until garlic is lightly browned. Using a low heat, add pheasant pieces, turning frequently until browned. Add white wine and tomato sauce. Bring to boil and add remaining ingredients. Add enough water to keep the pheasant from burning. Turn to low heat and cover. Allow to simmer for 20-30 minutes (depending on amount of pheasant). Serve on a bed of rice or pasta. Serves 3-5.

Kenneth L. Deal, Jr.
Fort Knox, Kentucky

Gus's Breast of Pheasant

2 whole pheasant
  breasts
1 egg with 1 tsp. water,
  whisked
2 cups fine bread
  crumbs
4 tbsp. olive oil
Butter
Salt and white pepper
2 cups seasoned medium
  white sauce

Bone and skin the breasts. Slice each breast into 2 or 3 equal-sized pieces. Season each piece with salt and white pepper. Dredge them in flour, dip them in the egg wash, and coat them in the bread crumbs. Cover and refrigerate for several hours or overnight. To cook, preheat non-stick skillet over medium-high heat. Add olive oil and a small pat of butter and heat briefly. Sauté the pieces for 2-3 minutes per side. Turn frequently until golden brown, not more than 6-7 minutes total cooking time. Remove and drain. Serve with a medium white sauce seasoned with chicken bouillon and white pepper. Serves 3-4.

Richard A. VonFeldt
Larned, Kansas

HONEY PHEASANT

1 pheasant, disjointed
4 tbsp. peanut oil
1 scallion, chopped
1 slice ginger root
1/2 cup dry sherry
2 tbsp. honey
1 tsp. salt

Heat oil, sauté ginger and scallion until brown, remove. Brown pheasant pieces. Remove excess oil. Add mixture of sherry and honey. Reduce heat, cover, simmer 1/2 hour. Salt to taste. Serves 2.

Richard Beardsley
Boulder, Colorado

LEMON-BAKED PHEASANT

1 or 2 pheasants,
   disjointed
Juice of 1 lemon
3 tbsp. honey
3 tbsp. butter
1 tsp. paprika
3/4 cup flour
Salt and pepper
1/2 cup peanut oil

Mix lemon juice, honey, and butter. Mix paprika, salt, and pepper and coat pheasant pieces with mixture. Let stand 30 minutes. Coat pheasant pieces with flour. Line pan with foil. Spread 1/2 cup oil over pan bottom. Place pheasant pieces skin side down in pan in one layer. Heat oven to 400 degrees; bake 30 minutes. Turn over; pour lemon mixture over pieces. Bake 20-30 minutes until done. Baste with lemon mixture during cooking. Serves 2-4.

Richard Beardsley
Boulder, Colorado

PHEASANT IN MUSHROOM GRAVY

1 pheasant, boned
1 can cream of
  mushroom soup
  (10³/₄ oz.)
1 tbsp. soy sauce
Seasoned salt to taste
Paprika

Place pheasant in baking dish. Mix soup, soy sauce, and seasoned salt in 2-cup measuring cup. Add in enough water to make 2 cups. Stir. Pour over pheasant. Sprinkle with paprika. Bake uncovered at 375 degrees for 1¹/₂ hours or until tender. Baste occasionally. Serve with rice or potatoes. Serves 2-3.

Anna D. Cook
Ft. Collins, Colorado

SMOTHERED SAGE GROUSE

3 grouse breasts
Flour
Salt
Pepper
Paprika
Margarine
2 cans beef broth
  (10 oz. each)
2 tbsp. lemon juice
1 onion, diced
2 whole cloves
3 bay leaves
4 peppercorns
¹/₂ cup red wine
  (optional)

Split and bone three breasts. Dredge breasts and thighs in seasoned flour (salt, pepper, and paprika). Brown in margarine. Add beef broth, lemon juice, and remaining ingredients except wine. Cook (simmer) in Dutch oven or slow cooker 3-4 hours. May add ¹/₂ cup red wine 30 minutes before serving. If desired, thicken gravy with 1-2 tbsp. cornstarch mixed with a small amount of water. Serves 3.

Harriet Parks
Alpine, Wyoming

Glazed Grouse Breast

**6 grouse breasts,
skinned**
¹/₂ cup honey
¹/₄ cup Heinz 57 sauce

Mix together honey and Heinz 57 to make a basting sauce. Cook grouse breasts on grill, lightly basting each one with glaze as you turn them over. Apply a thick coat of glaze the last few minutes of cooking time. Serves 4.

Debora Ann Petty
Columbia Falls, Montana

Sweet and Sour Grouse

4 grouse breasts, cubed
Cornstarch
Oil for frying
**1 can oriental vegetables
(14-16 oz.)**
**1 bag chow mein noodles
(17 oz.)**

Sweet and Sour Sauce:
3 tbsp. ketchup
4 tsp. vinegar
2 tbsp. sugar
¹/₄ cup brown sugar
1 tbsp. cornstarch
**¹/₄ cup onions, finely
chopped, or sweet
pickle relish**
²/₃ cup water

Coat grouse in cornstarch. Place in fry pan in ¹/₄-inch of hot oil. Brown. Drain grouse on paper towels. Set aside. Mix sweet and sour sauce. Cook until thick, add drained vegetables and meat. Cook only until meat is hot, stirring occasionally. Spoon over noodles and serve. Serves 4.

Debora Ann Petty
Columbia Falls, Montana

Sage Hen and Wild Rice Casserole

1 large sage hen
  (3 cups cubed meat)
2 stalks celery
1 onion, halved
Salt and pepper to taste
$^1/_2$ cup margarine
$^1/_2$ cup chopped onions
$^1/_4$ cup flour
4 oz. canned
  mushrooms, sliced
1$^1/_2$ cups half-and-half
1 tbsp. chopped, fresh
  parsley
1 pkg. seasoned wild and
  long grain rice mix
  (6 oz.)
Slivered almonds

Pressure cook sage hen (until tender, approximately 25 minutes) in water with celery, onion halves, and salt and pepper to taste. After pressure has gone down, remove meat and cool. Remove meat from bones and cube and set aside. Reserve broth. Cook the rice according to the package directions. Melt margarine; sauté onions; stir in the flour. Drain mushrooms, reserving broth; add mushrooms to the onion mixture. Add enough sage hen broth to mushroom broth to make 1$^1/_2$ cups of liquid; stir into the onions. Add half-and-half, parsley, and rice mix, plus 1$^1/_2$ tsp. salt and $^1/_4$ tsp. pepper. Put into greased 2-quart casserole. Sprinkle almonds on top. Bake covered at 250 degrees for 15-20 minutes. Uncover and bake 5-10 minutes more, or until very hot. (If the casserole has been refrigerated, it will take longer to heat.) If you don't have sage hen, try substituting any wild bird. Serves 6.

Suzette Horton
Idaho Falls, Idaho

Wild Duck a la Orange

2 wild ducks (whole,
    picked, cleaned, and
    readied to cook by
    the hunter)
1 onion, quartered

Glaze:
1 medium onion, sliced
    and separated into
    rings
2 tbsp. butter
2 tbsp. frozen orange
    juice concentrate,
    thawed
2 tbsp. honey
1 tbsp. lemon juice
$1/2$ tsp. ground ginger
$1/4$ tsp. allspice

Prepare orange glaze. Cook onion in butter until tender, but not brown. Stir in orange juice concentrate, honey, lemon juice, ginger, and allspice. Heat just to boiling. Place 2 quarters of onion in each duck cavity. Roast ducks in slow cooker. Cook for 8 hours or until joints move easily. The last hour, baste with orange glaze. Serves 4.

Suzette Horton
Idaho Falls, Idaho

Tempura Duck

1 duck, salted inside

TEMPURA BATTER:
2 eggs, beaten
¹/₂ cup flour
¹/₂ tsp. salt
¹/₂ cup milk
¹/₄ cup cornstarch
Oil for deep-frying

Mix eggs, flour, salt, milk, and cornstarch to make batter. Set aside. Steam duck 45 minutes. Cool. Remove meat from bones in chunky pieces. Dip pieces in batter, deep fry 1-2 minutes, until golden brown. Drain and serve with a lemon sauce. Serves 2-4.

Richard Beardsley
Boulder, Colorado

Roast Duck

4 whole, cleaned ducks
1 bunch celery
2 carrots
1 large onion
3-4 sprigs fresh
 rosemary or 2 tsp.
 dried rosemary
Salt and pepper
4 small roasting bags
 with ties
Flour

Rinse ducks and pat dry. In food processor, chop celery, carrots, and onion until they resemble the consistency of pickle relish. Pack each duck cavity tightly with this mixture. Sprinkle salt and pepper on outside of ducks. Poke a sprig of fresh rosemary inside each cavity, or sprinkle dried rosemary on outside of duck. Place each duck in a roaster bag and toss in 1 tsp. flour before closing. Cut a slit at top of each bag. Place ducks in shallow roasting pan and bake at 375 degrees for 1-1¹/₂ hours. To serve, cut ducks in half and eat with vegetable relish in cavity. Serves 8.

Luci Friday
Sacramento, California

CURRIED WILD DUCK OR GOOSE

2 large wild ducks
(3 lbs. each), split
in half
2 cans pineapple chunks
(8 oz. each)
$^1/_2$ cup pineapple juice
2 tbsp. orange
marmalade
2 tbsp. brown sugar
1 tbsp soy sauce
1 tsp. powdered ginger
$^1/_2$ tsp. powdered curry
$^1/_2$ tsp. powdered
mustard
Oven cooking bag

After you cut the ducks in half, set them on paper towels to drain. In an oven baking bag, put 1 tbsp. flour and shake. Mix together remaining ingredients. Put in bag with duck and shake to coat. Tie bag closed. Place in 9 x 13-inch glass dish. Microwave 35 minutes on high. One duck takes 24 minutes on high. Turn 3 times. In a conventional oven, bake at 350 degrees for 2 hours. Serves 4-6.

Salle Rice
Butte, Montana

WILD DUCK IN WINE SAUCE

2 wild ducks, quartered
4 tbsp. butter
4 tbsp. flour
2 cups chicken bouillon
  or broth
1 cup burgundy
1 medium chopped
  onion
2 bay leaves
1 tsp. celery salt
¹/₂ tsp. pepper
2 cups fresh mushrooms,
  sliced

Simmer ducks, covered, in small amount of salted water for 30 minutes, drain. In skillet, brown ducks in butter over high heat, then transfer to baking dish. Blend flour into butter, add broth, burgundy, onion, bay leaves, celery salt, and pepper. Cook and stir until thickened and bubbly. Add mushrooms. Pour over ducks. Cover and bake at 325 degrees for 2 hours or until tender. Add more burgundy if needed. Serves 4.

Helen Kadrmas
Plymouth, Minnesota

WILD DUCK IN RED CURRANT SAUCE

Duck breast fillets, 10-12
¹/₂ cup red wine
¹/₄ cup oil
¹/₄ cup soy sauce

SAUCE FOR DUCK:
1 cup red currant jelly
2 tbsp. Dijon mustard
1¹/₂ tsp. red wine vinegar
1 tsp. soy sauce
³/₄ tsp. Worcestershire
**   sauce**
¹/₄ tsp. cumin
¹/₈ tsp. pepper

Marinate fillets in wine, oil, and soy mixture for 3 hours. Broil until desired doneness. Heat sauce ingredients until melted. Stir and serve over duck. Serves 4-6.

Marge Derby
Modesto, California

Foundation Chicken

4 chicken breasts
1 can cream of
  chicken soup (10¾ oz.)
Chicken Shake 'n Bake
4 slices Swiss cheese

Place chicken in 9 x 9-inch pan and sprinkle heavily with Shake 'n Bake. Place sliced cheese on each breast. Cover with soup and bake covered at 350 degrees for 30-35 minutes, until browned. Serve with white rice. Serves 4.

Dianne Aaberg

State Fair Tenderloin

1 lb. turkey tenderloin,
  ¾-1-inch thick
¼ cup soy sauce
2 tbsp. vegetable oil
¼ cup dry sherry
2 tbsp. pure lemon juice
2 tbsp. dehydrated onion
¼ tsp. powdered ginger
Dash black pepper
Dash garlic salt

Blend all ingredients, except turkey, together in shallow pan for marinade. Add turkey. Cover and refrigerate for six hours, turning occasionally. Grill over hot coals, 6-8 minutes per side. Use marinade to baste occasionally. Turkey is done when no longer pink in center of meat. Slice into steaks. Serves 3-4.

Ann Porter
Pleasant Hill, Missouri

Marinated Wild Turkey Breast

1 lb. turkey breast,
   ³/₄-1-inch thick
1 tsp. dry mustard
2 tbsp. lemon juice
2 tbsp. soy sauce
2 tsp. salad oil

Remove skin and any fat from turkey. Combine remaining ingredients. Add turkey, turning to coat both sides. Cover and refrigerate at least 4 hours, turning occasionally. Grill over hot coals, 8-10 minutes. Serves 3-4.

Linda Henkes
McGregor, Iowa

Goose or Duck Meat Loaf

Goose or duck meat
Italian sausage
Meatloaf ingredients,
   your choice

Coarse grind goose or duck meat, using breast, thighs, and legs. Mix meat with equal amounts of Italian sausage. (Prepared hot sausage like Jimmy Dean's works well.) Now blend in your favorite meat loaf ingredients and let set in the refrigerator overnight. Pack mixture tightly into bread pans and bake in oven at 325 degrees for approximately 2 hours. While cooking, drain off moisture and grease that accumulates. Meat loaf may be reheated or sliced cold and used for sandwiches.

Tom Canape
Evergreen, Colorado

Morgan Hill Goose

1 goose breast, skinned
Salt and pepper
3 eggs
2 garlic cloves, crushed
2 tbsp. fresh parsley,
  chopped
1 cup seasoned bread
  crumbs
1 cup white wine
Butter or margarine

Cut goose breast into 1-inch cubes. Salt and pepper. Beat eggs. Add garlic and parsley. Pour over goose breast and marinate, covered, in the refrigerator for 4-8 hours. Remove from marinade and coat goose cubes with seasoned bread crumbs. Fry in butter until juices appear. Turn and cook on second side 2-3 minutes more. Put meat into baking dish and add wine. Bake 15-20 minutes in a 350-degree oven. Excellent as an appetizer or served as a main course with wild rice. Serves 2-4.

Bob Henke
Richland, Washington

GRILLED GOOSE BREAST

Goose breasts
Red table wine
Poultry seasonings
Butter
2 garlic cloves

Each goose breast will serve 2 people. Use only the breast of the goose. Bone, then marinate breasts in a red table wine. Refrigerate for at least 4-6 hours. Add poultry seasoning if desired. Prepare barbecue coals. Grill breast for 8-10 minutes per side; you want the meat rare to medium rare. Melt butter in sauce pan, add juice of 2 garlic cloves. Use to baste breasts as they cook. Place breasts on serving plate. Pour garlic butter over them. Slice on a diagonal; they will look and taste like tenderloin. Serve with French bread, rice pilaf, grilled tomatoes, or other vegetable.

NOTE: One easy way to marinate breasts: If you plan to freeze them, put breasts in heavy plastic freezer bag, pour red wine in, seal, and freeze. When you defrost, the wine will marinate meat.

Lyn Neel
Eugene, Oregon

GOOSE BREAST SAUTERNE

1 boneless goose breast
  per serving
¹/₂ cup sauterne wine
¹/₂ tsp. salt
¹/₄ tsp. pepper
¹/₂ tsp. garlic salt
¹/₂ cup flour
Vegetable oil for
  browning

Multiply all seasoning ingredients by the number of breasts being prepared. Cut the breasts in half and pound with a meat hammer to tenderize. Mix salt, pepper, garlic salt, and flour in a bag. Shake breasts in flour mixture to coat. Brown goose breasts very slowly in oil in a heavy skillet. Mix sauterne with equal amount of water and pour over meat. Cover and simmer until tender. Serve with cooked wild rice. Serves 2.

Anna D. Cook
Fort Collins, Colorado

TURKEY CREPE CASSEROLE

CREPES:

1 egg

1 cup milk

1 tbsp. butter, melted

1 cup sifted all-purpose
   flour

FILLING AND SAUCE:

1 cup finely diced
   cooked turkey or
   chicken

1/2 cup chopped cooked
   spinach, well drained

1 can condensed cream
   of chicken soup
   (10 1/2 oz.)

1/4 cup medium cracker
   crumbs

1/4 cup grated Parmesan
   cheese

1/4 cup chopped onion

1 cup milk

1/3 cup sliced almonds,
   toasted

To make crepes, beat egg to blend; add milk, butter, and flour; beat until smooth. Lightly grease a 6-inch skillet; heat. Pour 2 tbsp. batter into skillet; lift pan and tilt from side to side until batter covers bottom. Return to heat. When brown, flip to other side and cook briefly. Repeat with remaining batter. Makes 12 crepes.

FILLING: Mix turkey, spinach, half of the soup, cracker crumbs, cheese, and onion. Spoon a heaping tbsp. of filling on cooked side of each crepe; roll up. Arrange, seam side down, in greased, shallow baking dish.

SAUCE: Combine remaining soup with 1 cup milk; pour over crepes. Sprinkle with almonds. Bake at 350 degrees for 30 minutes. Drizzle with melted butter. Serves 6.

Donna Williams
La Porte, Texas

WILD TURKEY AND MUENSTER CASSEROLE

**Turkey breast meat,
    sliced**
I egg
Bread cumbs
Fresh mushrooms
Muenster cheese
Mozzarella cheese
Dry chicken soup mix

Dip sliced turkey in egg and bread crumbs and brown in oil in pan. Place in baking dish. Slice fresh mushrooms and cover the turkey. Grate muenster cheese and mozzarella cheese and cover well. Use 1 tsp. dry chicken soup mix with approximately ½ cup water and sprinkle over top. Bake at 350 degrees until cheese has melted and turns golden brown. Amounts depend on size of baking dish you are using. Also freezes well.

Elsie M. Bentley
Kamloops, British Columbia

LEMON MUSHROOM CHICKEN
(OR GROUSE OR PHEASANT)

**6-8 chicken breast halves
(you can skin and
bone them) or 1
whole chicken cut up,
or 3-4 grouse cut up,
or 1-2 pheasants
cut up**
**¹/₄-¹/₂ lb. fresh sliced
mushrooms**
**Garlic salt or garlic
powder**
**Margarine or butter,
2 tbsp. at a time as
needed**
¹/₃-¹/₂ cup lemon juice
³/₄ cup white wine
Paprika

Sauté mushrooms in butter and a sprinkling of garlic salt or powder until limp. Remove from pan. Add more butter and brown breasts. Sprinkle with a little garlic powder and paprika. Put mushrooms back in with chicken, add lemon juice and white wine. Turn heat to simmer and cover. Simmer for about 1 hour for chicken and 1¹/₂ hours for grouse or pheasant. Take cover off and raise heat to reduce liquid until it gets thick and turns a darker color. Serve with rice. Serves 6-8.

Linda Ward
Missoula, Montana

CHICKEN ENCHILADAS

1 medium onion,
   chopped
2-3 tbsp. butter
1 can cream of chicken
   soup (10³/₄ oz.)
1 can cream of
   mushroom soup
   (10³/₄ oz.)
1 can chicken broth
   (10¹/₂ oz.)
1 or 1¹/₂ small cans
   chopped green chilies
   (4 oz.)
1 chicken (3 lb.), cooked,
   skinned, boned, and
   chopped
1 pkg. corn tortillas
   (broken into pieces)
1 lb. cheddar cheese,
   grated

Brown onion in butter. Combine onion with soups, chicken broth, green chilies, and pieces of chicken. Mix well and heat; do not boil. Place in 13 x 9 x 2-inch greased casserole pan as follows: Put a little of the sauce in the bottom of the pan, then a layer of tortillas, then a layer of sauce. Repeat until filled and end with cheese. Freezes well and can be frozen at this point, uncooked. Bake at 350 degrees for 45 minutes or until hot and bubbly. Serves 8.

Sue Gooding
Albuquerque, New Mexico

Wild Turkey Casserole

2-3 lb. wild turkey, boned and skinned, or 3-4 lb. fryer chicken
¹/₄ cup peanut oil
1 can cream of mushroom soup (10³/₄ oz.)
1 can cream of celery soup (10³/₄ oz.)
1 can cream of chicken soup (10³/₄ oz.)
³/₄ cup white wine
2 cups shredded cheddar cheese
1 small pkg. sliced almonds (2 oz.)

Cut the white and dark meat of the turkey into small portions and season with salt and pepper. Brown turkey in oil and place in 9 x 13-inch pan. Combine undiluted soups, wine, and 1¹/₂ cups cheese. Stir until mixed. Pour over turkey. Sprinkle remaining cheese and almonds over top. Cover with foil and bake 1 hour at 375 degrees. Serve with cooked noodles. Serves 6-8.

Sharon Robertson
Kansas City, Kansas

MEAT

Elk Loin Chops

4 elk loin chops
1/3 cup salad oil
3 tbsp. soy sauce
2 tbsp. ketchup
2 cloves garlic, minced
1 tbsp. vinegar
1/4 tsp. pepper

Mix together everything but the meat. Add meat, marinate for 3-4 hours covered in refrigerator. Remove from marinade and grill over medium coals on barbecue.

Harriett Parks
Alpine, Wyoming

Breaded Venison Chops

6 venison chops
1 egg
2 tbsp. water
Dry cracker meal
1 can cream of
   mushroom soup
   (10³/4 oz.) diluted
   with 1/2 can water
Poultry seasoning
   to taste
Salt and pepper to taste

Sprinkle chops with salt, pepper, and poultry seasoning. Dip into beaten egg diluted with water. Coat well with dry cracker meal. Brown on both sides. Add soup, cover, and simmer 45 minutes or until tender. Serves 6.

Robert and Michele Sandness
LaMoure, North Dakota

VENISON RICE CASSEROLE

6 venison boneless chops
1 tbsp. olive oil
2 cups long cooking rice
1 can of beef bouillon
   (10 oz.)
¹/₂ cup water
2 tbsp. paprika
1 large onion, chopped

Brown chops in oil in frying pan. Remove chops from pan and place in 2-quart casserole dish. Add onion and paprika to frying pan. Sauté onion until brown. Add liquid and heat until boiling. Spread rice evenly over chops and pour liquid over all. Cover casserole dish and bake at 350 degrees for 60 minutes. Serves 6.

Patti Pease
Duarte, California

BARBECUE VENISON

4 venison chops
¹/₄ tsp. onion salt
¹/₂ tsp. salt
¹/₄ tsp. pepper
3 tbsp. flour
4 tbsp. oil
¹/₂ cup ketchup
¹/₄ cup vinegar
¹/₂ tsp. garlic powder
1 tsp. liquid smoke
1 tsp. Worcestershire
Dash of Tabasco

In bowl mix onion, salt, pepper, and flour. Coat chops with mixture and fry in oil until brown. Mix remaining ingredients and pour over browned chops. Cover and simmer until tender. Serves 4.

Alice Taylor
Eagle, Idaho

Wine-sauced Elk Round Steak

1 1/2 lb. elk round steak
2 tbsp. flour
1/2 tsp. salt
Dash of pepper
2 tbsp. oil
1/2 cup dry red wine
1/4 cup water
1 can sliced mushrooms
   (13 oz.)
1/4 cup chopped onion
1 tbsp. snipped parsley
1/4 tsp. salt
1/4 tsp. dry basil
1 tbsp. cornstarch
1/4 cup water

Roll steak in flour, salt, and pepper. Brown in oil. Combine remaining ingredients, except cornstarch and water. Pour over meat in an oven baking dish. Cover. Bake at 350 degrees until meat is tender. Thicken juices with cornstarch mixed with water and cook until smooth and thickened. Serves 4-6.

Sandy Rabe

Elk Swiss Steak

2 lbs. elk steak, cut into
   serving pieces
Flour
Cooking oil
1 pkg. dry onion soup
   mix
2 bay leaves
2 tsp. spaghetti sauce
   seasoning
1 1/2 cups dry red wine
1 can tomato sauce
   (16 oz.)

Flour meat. Brown in oil. Drain off oil. Combine soup mix, seasoning, wine, and tomato sauce. Pour over meat. Bring to boil, then simmer covered until tender. If sauce gets too thick, add more wine or water. (I cook this in a crock pot; dinner is ready when I get home.) Serve on noodles with salad and French bread. Serves 6-8.

Bernis Wagner
Roseburg, Washington

Deviled Swiss Steak

2 lbs. round steak (elk,
   moose, or venison)
1 tbsp. dry mustard
1/2 tsp. pepper
4 tbsp. flour
1-2 tbsp. cooking oil
1 cup water
1 tsp. beef bouillon
   granules
1 tbsp. Worcestershire
   sauce
2 cans mushrooms
   (6 oz. each)

Combine mustard, pepper, and flour. Cut steak into serving size pieces, dredge in flour, mustard, and pepper mixture, and brown in oil. Add water, bouillon granules, Worcestershire sauce, and mushrooms. Cover and simmer 30 minutes or until tender. Serves 6-8.

Linda Henkes
McGregor, Iowa

RAWHIDE'S SWISS ELK STEAK

**2 lbs. elk round steak,
1-inch thick
4 tbsp. flour
1 tsp. dry mustard
2 tsp. salt
1/4 tsp. pepper
2 tbsp. cooking oil
2 cups sliced onions
1 clove garlic,
   finely chopped
1/2 cup water
1/2 cup chili sauce**

Mix dry seasonings with flour.
Dredge meat in the flour mixture.
Heat oil in pan and brown steak. Add
remaining ingredients and simmer
until tender (1 hour or more). Serves 6.

*Beverly Hyde
Post Falls, Idaho*

ELK SUPREME

**1 1/2 lbs. elk steak
4 slices bacon, cut
   in 1-inch pieces
1/4 cup onion, chopped
1 can cream of
   mushroom soup
   (10 1/2 oz.)
1/3 cup red wine
Salt and pepper to taste
Flour (to coat elk)**

In frying pan, brown bacon pieces
with onion (not crisp). Flour elk steaks
and add to frying pan with bacon and
onion. Brown steaks on both sides. In
small bowl, mix mushroom soup and
wine. Pour over steaks in frying pan and
blend well. Add salt and pepper. Cover
and cook on very low, stirring
occasionally. Cook 1 hour or until
tender. Serves 4.

*Cara Davis
Yreka, California*

German Venison Steak

I lb. venison steak, cut
    into 3 or 4 pieces
Whole small dill pickles
2 tbsp. olive oil
2 peeled and minced
    shallots
I can beef broth (10 oz.)
I bay leaf
I tsp. dried thyme
6 whole juniper berries
I cup red wine
Salt and pepper to taste
¼ cup thinly sliced
    mushrooms

Place pickle on each venison steak, roll up and secure with a toothpick. Using cast iron skillet, brown venison steaks in 1 tbsp. oil. Remove steaks and sauté shallots, adding the remaining oil if necessary. Put steaks back in pan and add beef broth, bay leaf, thyme, and juniper berries. Boil down to 3 tbsp. Add red wine and boil down to half the amount. Remove juniper berries and bay leaf. Season with salt and pepper if desired. Stir in mushrooms and cool briefly. To serve, spoon some of the sauce onto 3 or 4 plates, place steak in middle of sauce and spoon balance of sauce over steaks. Serves 3-4.

Cheri Eby
Gunnison, Colorado

VENISON PEPPER STEAK

1 lb. venison, elk, or
   moose steak
1 tbsp. paprika
2 tbsp. butter or
   margarine
2 cloves garlic, crushed
1 1/2 cups venison or beef
   broth
1 cup sliced green
   onions
2 green peppers, cut in
   strips
2 tbsp. cornstarch
1/4 cup water
1/8 cup soy sauce
   (increase to 1/4 cup
   if you want it more
   salty)
2 large fresh tomatoes,
   cut in eighths

Cut the steak into strips about
1/2-inch thick. Sprinkle steak with
paprika and allow to stand while
preparing other ingredients. Using a
large skillet, brown steaks in butter.
Add garlic and broth. Cover and simmer
30-45 minutes or until tender. Stir in
onions and green peppers. Cover and
cook 10 minutes more or until onions
and peppers are just tender. Blend
cornstarch, water, and soy sauce. Stir
into meat mixture. Cook, stirring, until
clear and thickened (about 2 minutes).
Add tomatoes and stir gently. Heat until
tomatoes are hot. Serve over bed of hot
cooked rice. Makes 3-6 servings,
depending on appetites!

Cathy Malison
Bordentown, New Jersey

CURRIED ELK AND VEGETABLES

1 lb. elk round steak
2 small onions
1 cup sugar snap peas
   (or snow peas)
1/4 tsp. cayenne pepper
1/4 tsp. ground ginger
1/2 tsp. sugar
1 tbsp. soy sauce
1 tbsp. curry powder
1/2 cup beef stock
2 tbsp. vegetable oil
2 tsp. cornstarch
1 tbsp. water

Cut the steak in 1$^{1}/_{2}$-2-inch strips, then slice thinly on the diagonal. Cut onions in quarters and separate the layers. Combine cayenne, ginger, sugar, soy sauce, curry powder, and beef stock and set aside. Heat oil in a large skillet. Sauté steak in hot oil until it is almost completely browned. Push steak to side of pan. Add onions and sugar snap peas and sauté about 1 minute. Mix steak with vegetables and pour stock mixture over all. Cook, stirring, about 2 minutes. Stir cornstarch and water together and blend into liquid. Cook, stirring, until smooth and slightly thickened. Serve over rice. Serves 4.

Kelly Coleman
Loveland, Colorado

ELK STEAK "MARY JANE"

2 lbs. boneless sirloin elk, deer, or moose steak

2 tbsp. (or more as needed) butter

Pepper (fresh or coarse ground)

Dry mustard

4 tbsp. Worcestershire sauce

4-6 tbsp. lemon juice

1/2 cup fresh chives, chopped

Cut steaks or pound them to 1/2-inch thick at most. Sprinkle with pepper and mustard on both sides. Brown in butter until medium rare and remove to warm plate. Add Worcestershire sauce, lemon juice, and chives to pan and reduce until sauce thickens. If you'd like to use thicker steaks, you can put them back in with the sauce and simmer until medium rare. Serves 4-6.

Linda Ward
Missoula, Montana

ELK WITH SCOTCH SAUCE

2 tbsp. butter

4 elk steaks, ¹/₂-inch
  thick (no thicker)

¹/₄ cup finely chopped
  shallots

6 juniper berries
  (crushed)

¹/₄ cup Scotch whiskey

2 tbsp. lemon juice

³/₄ cup orange juice
  (fresh)

2 tbsp. red currant jelly
  or mint jelly
  (for variety)

1 tsp. dry English
  mustard mixed with
  2 tsp. water

2 tsp. cornstarch

In a heavy skillet melt one tablespoon butter over medium heat. Sauté steaks, 2¹/₂ minutes per side until brown on outside and pink on inside. Remove steaks to a heated serving platter. Cover with foil to keep warm. In same skillet melt remaining butter and sauté shallots and juniper berries over medium heat for 3 minutes. Add scotch, bring to boil, and ignite with match. When flame subsides, stir in orange juice, lemon juice, jelly, and mustard. Return to light boil for 3 minutes. Combine cornstarch with 2-3 tbsp. water. Mix and stir into sauce. Cook until it starts to thicken. Serve over elk steaks. Serves 4.

Richard Dimbat
Bend, Oregon

ELK STRIPS AND BROCCOLI

1 lb. elk steak

¼ tsp. garlic powder

1 tsp. salt

1 tsp. dried ginger

6 tsp. cornstarch

½ tsp. 5-spice powder

½ lb. broccoli

2 tsp. cornstarch

2 tbsp. water

2 tbsp. soy sauce

4 tbsp. oil

Cut elk in very thin slices. Mix together salt, garlic, and ginger. Combine with elk. Toss elk with 2 tsp. cornstarch and 5-spice powder. Remove tough part of stem and cut broccoli into small bite-sized pieces. Mix remaining cornstarch, water, and soy sauce. Set aside. Heat oil in large fry pan. Sauté elk for 2-4 minutes. Add broccoli and stir fry 5 minutes. Stir in cornstarch mixture, cook until thick. Serve immediately on a bed of rice. Serves 4-6.

Karen Jean Funk

Ten Sleep, Wyoming

FINGER STEAKS

1 cup flour
**Seasoning salt, garlic
powder, onion
powder, and pepper
(to taste)**
1 egg
³/₄ cup milk
**Cracker crumbs
(¹/₂ of a 1 lb. box—
approximately 80
crackers)**
**Your favorite steak
(1¹/₂-2 lbs.), cut in
bite-sized (or larger)
pieces**
Oil for deep fat frying

Mix flour and seasonings together and set aside. In separate bowl, beat 1 egg and ³/₄ cup milk. Pound flour mixture into steaks before cutting into bite-sized (or larger) pieces, then dip in egg mixture and roll in cracker crumbs. Put enough oil in frying pan to float the steaks. Cook on one side and then turn over, or use a deep fat fryer and cook 5-7 minutes at 375 degrees. Drain.

NOTE: Rick Anzalone of Chehalis, Washington uses equal parts of bread crumbs and Parmesan cheese instead of cracker crumbs.

Sue R. Ellis
Moscow, Idaho

Buck 'n' Bull Grilled Tenderloin

1 elk or deer tenderloin, approximately 12 inches long
1 bottle Heinz 57 steak sauce
1 bottle Lea & Perrins Worcestershire sauce
8 tbsp. butter

Trim all excess white fat or any white-colored meat from the whole tenderloin. (Rule is: "if it's white, don't eat it"). Wash tenderloin well and place in a rectangular dish approximately 12 inches long x 4 inches deep. In a small mixing bowl, mix equal amounts of Heinz 57 steak sauce and Lea & Perrins Worcestershire sauce. Prepare enough mix so as to pour the entire mixture over the tenderloin and leave approximately $1/2$ inch of excess mixture in the bottom of the dish. Cover and refrigerate 8-12 hours. Periodically turn.

Remove from the refrigerator. Prepare charcoal grill for cooking. Melt butter for basting or use excess marinade to do so. Place meat on grill. Baste often. Once the meat is grilled as desired, cut it into medallions or fillet-sized steaks, which can be served with bernaise sauce or barbecue sauce.

Glen E. Stinson
Dallas, Georgia

Mountain Lion Medallions

**1-2 mountain lion
backstraps**
¹/₂ cup flour
¹/₂ tsp. salt
¹/₄ tsp. pepper
**1 tbsp. butter flavored
Crisco**

SAUCE:
**8 oz. sliced fresh
mushrooms**
2-4 tbsp. butter
1 tbsp. brandy
**1 tsp. garlic juice
or powder**
Dash of salt and pepper
Dried dill

ROUX:
¹/₄ cup butter
2 tbsp. flour
1 cup whipping cream

Cut backstraps into ¹/₂-inch rounds. Should yield 9-18 rounds. Dredge in flour, salt, and pepper mixture. Fry in Crisco over medium heat until golden, slightly crisp with no pink juice. Create sauce while frying medallions. Sauté mushrooms in butter until brown colored. Add garlic, salt, and brandy. Cook until liquid is reduced. Make roux by heating butter in saucepan. Stir in flour when butter is melted. Let cook briefly. Whisk in cream. Let cook until thickened. Sauce should be gravy consistency. Thin with milk if needed. Add mushrooms, salt, and pepper to taste. Serve sauce over medallions. Sprinkle dried dill on sauce before serving. Serves 4-6.

Rita Suminski
Grants, New Mexico

Steaks on the Grill

I backstrap loin, sliced
  1 1/2-inch thick
Lawry's salt
Onion powder
Black pepper
Garlic powder
Accent
Butter

Heavily season each steak. Refrigerate a few hours so meat absorbs seasoning. Brown on a hot grill a few minutes on each side. Brush on butter on each side and serve when rare to medium. (The longer you cook, the dryer and tougher the meat will be.)

John Zanon
Norway, Michigan

Barbecued Elk Steaks

3-4 lbs. elk steaks
I tbsp. water
2 tbsp. chablis wine
1/4 cup oil
I pkg. Schilling meat
  marinade

Place steaks in marinating dish and pierce with a fork. Combine remaining ingredients and pour over steaks. Allow to stand at least 15 minutes, but an hour is best. Grill to desired doneness. This marinade can be used on many cuts of meat.

VARIATIONS: Paul Robinson, Providence, Utah, adds these ingredients to his marinade: soy sauce, steak sauce, fruit juice, or brown sugar.

Linda Padgett
Washougal, Washington

Elk Steak in Wine Caper Sauce

4 tender steaks or chops
Prepared Dijon mustard
3 tbsp. margarine
  or butter
¼ cup whipping cream
3-4 tbsp. capers
1 cup white wine

Spread steaks with mustard on both sides and brown in skillet with the butter, about 3 minutes on each side or until medium rare. (I usually turn steaks when red juices start seeping out top of steaks, then remove from pan when it does the same on the other side.) Remove from pan and keep warm. Add capers and wine to pan, simmer to reduce slightly, then add cream. Heat through and pour over steaks.

Linda Ward
Missoula, Montana

SAVORY ELK STEAK

Steak for six
3 tbsp. soy sauce
1 tbsp. minced garlic
1 tsp. ground cumin
¹/₈ tsp. freshly ground pepper
¹/₄ cup margarine for sautéing steaks

MUSHROOM SAUCE:
1 lb. fresh mushrooms, sliced
2-4 tbsp. margarine
2 tbsp. white wine or water
¹/₈ tsp. each: cumin, powdered garlic, pepper, and salt

Mix soy sauce, garlic, cumin, and pepper with a small whisk or fork; spread mixture evenly over steak; set aside. Sauté mushrooms in margarine; add wine and sprinkle with seasonings. Cook briefly. In another pan sauté steaks in margarine (or grill) to desired doneness; top with mushroom sauce. Serves 6.

Miriam L. Jones
Eugene, Oregon

ELK MEDALLIONS WITH CREME DIJON

3 lbs. elk tenderloin
1 tbsp. garlic, minced
³/₄ cup soy sauce
³/₄ cup Worcestershire
sauce
2 celery stalks with
leaves, cut into thirds
1 medium onion,
quartered
¹/₂ cup beef stock
¹/₂ tsp. salt
¹/₄ tsp. pepper
¹/₂ tsp. lemon pepper

SAUCE:
6 tbsp. butter
¹/₄ cup flour
5 green onions, chopped
2 cups fresh mushrooms,
sliced
1 cup chicken stock
¹/₄ cup white wine
1 pint heavy cream
1 tbsp. prepared Dijon
mustard

Rub garlic on tenderloin. Put in baking pan. Mix together soy sauce and Worcestershire sauce. Pour over tenderloin, cover and marinate overnight in refrigerator. Drain. Place tenderloin in baking pan, top with celery, onions, beef stock, and seasonings. Bake at 350 degrees for 30 minutes or to desired doneness. In sauce pan, melt butter on medium heat. Add green onions and mushrooms, cook 5 minutes until soft. Add flour, stir well. Cook 1-2 minutes. Add chicken stock, wine, and stir to mix. Cook until slightly thickened. Add cream and mustard, stirring until creamy and warm throughout. Season to taste with salt. Carve meat, pour sauce over top. Serves 8.

Ron Bennett
Greeley, Colorado

MUSTARD-COATED ELK ROAST

1 1/2 tbsp. Hungarian
  sweet paprika
1 tbsp. crushed black
  peppercorns
1 tbsp. coarse salt
  (optional)
1 tbsp. dry oregano,
  crumbled
1 tbsp. dry thyme,
  crumbled
2 tsp. prepared Dijon
  mustard
2 tbsp. grated onion
2 garlic cloves, chopped
4 1/2 lb. roast, patted dry

Mix dry spices in a small bowl. Mix mustard, onion, and garlic in another small bowl. Rub mustard mixture over roast. Sprinkle with spice mixture; cover and refrigerate overnight. Let stand no more than 2 hours at room temperature before baking or barbecuing.

Prepare barbecue (high heat). Spread hot coals to outside edge and place rectangular aluminum pan on center of coals. Place roast on rack above pan. Cover with grill lid and cook until meat thermometer inserted in center of roast registers 140-150 degrees for medium-rare, about 2 hours. Transfer to platter, tent with foil and let stand 10 minutes before slicing.

Set oven at 350 degrees. Let meat "brown" about 20 minutes. Tent with foil to prevent drying. Turn to 325 degrees for about an hour, then 300 degrees for remaining time, depending on size and degree of doneness desired.

Mary Hughes
Glide, Oregon

Lemon-marinated Wild Game Roast

1 small roast (elk, venison, antelope, or moose)
½ cup lemon juice
⅓ cup salad oil
4 tbsp. sliced green onions
4 tsp. sugar
1½ tsp. salt
1 tsp. Worcestershire sauce
1 tsp. prepared mustard
⅛ tsp. pepper

Place roast in baking dish. Combine remaining ingredients and pour over roast. Cover and refrigerate 3-4 hours or overnight, turning roast several times. Remove roast from marinade and grill over medium-hot coals. Carve across grain.

NOTE: For grilling tips see previous "Mustard-coated Elk" recipe from Mary Hughes.

Harriett Parks
Alpine, Wyoming

OYSTER SAUCE ROAST

4-5 lb. deer or elk roast
2 tbsp. soy sauce
1 tbsp. oyster sauce
2 tbsp. dry sherry
3 cloves garlic, pressed
2 tbsp. cornstarch
Salt and pepper to taste

Preheat oven to 450 degrees. Mix together all ingredients except roast. Coat roast with part of oyster sauce mixture. Place roast on rack above foil in oven. Cook 15 minutes. Reduce heat to 325 degrees. Continue basting with remaining sauce mix while roast cooks. Cook until medium rare (about 20 minutes per pound.)

NOTE: Sauce can also be used to marinate steaks which are then grilled or broiled.

Richard Beardsley
Boulder, Colorado

COFFEE CHUCK ROAST

3-5 lb. chuck roast
1 pot cold day-old coffee
Salt and pepper to taste

Place roast in clay cooking pot or Pyrex pot with lid. Pour coffee over roast. Sprinkle with salt and pepper. Bake at 175 degrees for 8-10 hours. Incredibly tender and deliciously moist. It does not taste like coffee.

Cindi Bratvoid
Hamilton, Montana

ELK ROAST

4-7 lb. rump or sirloin
   roast
Flour
Oil
4 onions, sliced
3 carrots, sliced
2 stalks celery, sliced

MARINADE:
3 beef bouillon cubes
   dissolved in $\frac{1}{2}$ cup
   hot water
3 cups hearty red wine
   (merlot or cabernet)
$\frac{1}{4}$ cup garlic vinegar
1 tsp. powdered cloves
1 tbsp. dry thyme
2 tbsp. dry rosemary
1 tbsp. dry sage
$\frac{1}{2}$ tsp. pepper
$\frac{1}{4}$ tsp. cinnamon
$\frac{1}{4}$ tsp. ground ginger
2 bay leaves
2 tsp. lemon juice
4-6 cloves fresh garlic

GRAVY:
2 tbsp. flour
$\frac{1}{8}$ cup milk
$\frac{1}{8}$ cup water

Mix marinade ingredients together, bring to a full boil, and then cool completely before adding the elk roast. Marinate the elk roast 8-24 hours in the refrigerator, turning several times. Remove and pat dry with paper towels. Cut the garlic cloves into thirds (depending on the size of the garlic). Make cuts along the elk roast with a knife 1-2 inches deep and insert the sliced garlic into the slits. Roll the roast in flour and brown in vegetable oil or shortening in a Dutch oven or metal casserole. Add the marinade and sliced vegetables and, if you have the room, throw in enough red potatoes to feed your dinner guests.

Cook elk roast at 325 degrees until meat reaches desired doneness. In my experience, using a meat thermometer is essential in such cooking, as over-cooking a fine piece of meat is a crime, or at least it should be. Remove elk roast and vegetables from the Dutch oven and use remaining juices and fluid to make gravy. Shake flour, milk and water together and stir into pan juices. Cook until smooth and thickened. Homemade cornbread or biscuits are definitely to be considered with this meal.

James E. Pinch
Bellevue, Washington

SPICED ROAST

3 lb. roast
¹/₂ tsp. each of
  cinnamon, ground
  cloves, black pepper
Pinch dried nutmeg,
  dried thyme, dried
  marjoram, dried
  rosemary, and salt
2 tbsp. butter plus 1
  tbsp. oil
12-14 little white onions,
  peeled and cut with X
  at root end
1 tsp. sugar
4 tbsp. dry marsala wine
1 cup broth
1 bay leaf

Mix all herbs and spices, except bay leaf, in a bowl. Rub the roast with this mix. Heat the butter and oil in a stove-top casserole. Add roast and brown. Lower heat and add onions, brown a little, and sprinkle on sugar. Cook and stir for 5 minutes, add wine and let it evaporate. Add broth and bay leaf, cover, and continue cooking over low heat, turning often and adding more broth or water until meat is done (about 1³/₄ hours). Don't let roast dry out—keep adding liquid as necessary.

Joan Dublanko
Delta, British Columbia

Deer or Elk Pot Roast

3 lb. elk or venison roast
2 cloves garlic, minced
2 tsp. Worcestershire
sauce
¹/₂ cup lemon juice
¹/₂ tsp. dried tarragon
Salt and pepper
(Johnny's Seasoning is
good) to taste
1 can V-8 juice (16 oz.)
2 bay leaves
1 small onion, sliced

Combine all ingredients, except roast, for marinade. Pour over roast, cover, and refrigerate overnight. Turn occasionally. Next day add a little water as you would for a beef roast. Put 4 strips of bacon on top. Cover. Bake at 325 degrees for 2 hours or until tender.

Salle Rice
Butte, Montana

ITALIAN GAME POT ROAST

5 lb. elk or deer roast
3 tbsp. olive oil
1 qt. canned tomatoes
2 stalks celery, sliced
2 large onions, sliced
1 bell pepper, sliced
6 cloves garlic, sliced
1 small can ripe olives,
    sliced (3 oz.)
2 bay leaves, whole
1 tsp. sweet basil
Salt and pepper to taste
Cornstarch to thicken
Potatoes, optional
Carrots, optional

Brown roast in olive oil, add all ingredients except cornstarch, potatoes, and carrots. Cover and cook on top of stove until meat is tender, approximately 3-4 hours. Add cornstarch mixed with small amount of water if more thickness is desired. Add potatoes and carrots if desired and cook until they are done. Can be served as is or over mashed potatoes or rice. Serves 12.

Diana D. Noel
Vernal, Utah

ALICE'S QUICK ELK ROAST

2 lb. elk roast
1 can cream of
    mushroom soup
    (10³/₄ oz.)
1 pkg. dry onion soup
    mix
1 cup red wine
Fresh mushrooms and
    onions, sliced
Oil for browning

Sear elk roast in skillet. Put in crock pot on low. Add cream of mushroom soup and onion soup mix. Add one cup red wine. Cook in crock pot for 6 hours. Add mushrooms and onions. Cook one more hour.

VARIATION: Roger and Linda Witter, McGregor, Iowa, substitute one can of Pepsi for the red wine. Their recipe is cooked in a 325-degree oven, uncovered, until tender.

Alice Taylor
Eagle, Idaho

BARBECUED ELK ROAST

4 lb. elk roast
Salt and pepper
3 tbsp. fat or oil
3 cloves garlic, chopped
1 stalk celery, chopped
6 tbsp. vinegar
3 tbsp. ketchup
3 tbsp. Worcestershire
   sauce
2 tbsp. flour
3 tbsp. water

Season roast with salt and pepper. Melt fat in heavy pan; add roast and brown slowly on all sides. Add garlic and celery. Combine vinegar, ketchup, and Worcestershire sauce in a 1 cup measure. Add water to make 1 cup of liquid. Pour over roast; cover and cook slowly on top of stove about 2 hours or until tender. Remove roast. Stir together flour and water and add to pan juice. Cook to make a smooth thickened gravy. Serves 6.

Cheryn E. Bordonaro
Littleton, Colorado

BARBECUED ELK POT ROAST

4-6 lbs. arm roast or top
   round elk meat
2 cups water
1 cup chopped onion
2 stalks of celery,
   chopped

BARBECUE SAUCE:
1 tbsp. lemon juice
2 tbsp brown sugar
1 tbsp Worcestershire
   sauce
1 tbsp vinegar
1 bottle ketchup (32 oz.)
1 cup water

In large roasting pan put roast, water, and chopped vegetables. Add your favorite seasonings. Cover and bake at 350 degrees for 4 hours. Cool 1 hour. Pick meat apart; cut off and discard all fat. Reserve meat drippings for sauce. Combine sauce ingredients in saucepan. Bring to a simmer, then add to roast drippings and bake at 325 degrees for 1 hour. Serve sauce alongside meat. Delicious served with potato salad and baked beans. Great for picnics.

Cindy Stoeckmann

Red Simmered Pot Roast

3 lb. chuck roast,
  1¹/₂-inches thick
  (elk, moose, or
  venison)
1 tbsp. vegetable oil
¹/₂ cup stir-fry sauce
¹/₂ cup burgundy wine
¹/₂ lb. fresh mushrooms
  (canned may be
  substituted)
1 tbsp. cornstarch
¹/₄ cup water

Brown meat on both sides in hot oil in Dutch oven or large skillet. Combine stir-fry sauce and wine; pour over meat. Cover, reduce heat, and simmer about 2 hours. Add mushrooms and simmer, covered, 15 minutes longer or until meat is tender. Combine cornstarch and water, set aside. Remove meat to serving platter; add cornstarch mixture to pan drippings. Cook, stirring, until slightly thickened. Cut meat across grain and serve with hot mushroom gravy.

Linda Henkes
McGregor, Iowa

ORANGE VENISON ROAST

Medium venison roast
1 slice bacon, cut in
   small pieces
2 garlic cloves, smashed
Oil for browning
1 bay leaf
2 whole cloves
1 cup orange juice
Salt and pepper to taste

Cut small slits in meat and insert bacon and garlic. Season roast with salt and pepper. Sear meat in small amount of oil. Place in roasting pan and top with bay leaf and cloves. Roast in 325-degree oven, until done, while basting frequently with orange juice. Use meat thermometer to get desired doneness.

Les Roberts
Eugene, Oregon

ELK SAUERBRATEN

4-5 lb. elk chuck roast
2 tsp. salt
¹/₄ tsp. black pepper
¹/₂ tsp. MSG
2 cups water
2 cups red wine vinegar
¹/₂ cup diced onion
3 bay leaves
¹/₄ tsp. dried thyme
12 peppercorns
6 whole cloves
2 tbsp. celery flakes
1 tsp. mustard seed
1 large carrot, sliced
¹/₄ cup sugar
Flour
2 tbsp. cooking oil
18 gingersnaps, crushed
¹/₄ cup seedless raisins

Rub roast all over with salt, pepper, and MSG. Place in large glass or ceramic container with vinegar, onions, bay leaves, peppercorns, cloves, celery flakes, thyme, mustard seed, carrot, sugar, and water. Add only enough water to completely immerse the meat. Cover and marinate in refrigerator for 3 days, turning occasionally. When ready to cook, remove from marinade, pat dry, and dust all over with flour. Brown on all sides in hot cooking oil, drain, and place in roasting pan. Pour in reserved marinade and bake uncovered in oven for 3 hours at 325 degrees. Remove roast to a platter, cover, and place in turned-off warm oven.

Strain marinade liquid into large saucepan, bring to simmer, and add raisins and gingersnaps. Simmer and stir until gravy thickens. Slice meat thin on serving platter and pour gravy over it. Reserve side dish of hot gravy for dipping. Serves 8-10.

This dish is equally good if refrigerated in gravy, then reheated later.

Jim Roeland
Phelps, New York

ROAST BEAR

8 lb. bear roast
Water
3-4 medium onions,
sliced
1 clove garlic
Salt and pepper to taste
Bacon drippings

Use about an 8 lb. roast from the rump of a bear. Cover with cold water, add onions, and let soak about 4 hours. Remove from water and wipe dry. Cut garlic into small pieces and, using a sharp knife to make holes, force garlic deep into the meat. Get garlic as near the bone as possible. Season with salt and pepper. Brown in hot bacon drippings. Bake in open pan for 3 hours at 325 degrees, turning the meat several times while cooking.

Remember bear meat must be cooked until well done, the same as pork, as it is subject to trichinae contamination. Thorough cooking kills trichinae and makes the meat safe for consumption.

Fred Topil
Rising City, Nebraska

BOAR ROAST WITH PRUNES AND APPLES

3 to 4 lb. boar roast
1 clove garlic, slivered
1 medium onion, sliced
1 cup white wine
1/2 cup buttermilk
10-12 peppercorns
2 tbsp. cooking oil
1/4 cup flour
1 tbsp. Mrs. Dash
1/2 cup pitted prunes
2 medium Granny Smith
  apples, sliced
2 tbsp. flour
1/4 cup water
Oil for browning

Put roast in a large container. Cut slits along side of roast and stuff sliced garlic in each slit. Add the sliced onion, wine, buttermilk, and peppercorns; cover and marinate in refrigerator for 3-5 days. Remove boar from marinade and dry with paper towel. Mix flour and Mrs. Dash together and coat boar roast on all sides. Brown boar in oil in deep Dutch oven. Add marinade mixture and bring to boil. Cook on low heat about 2-2 1/2 hours. Add prunes and apples and simmer for another 10 minutes. Thicken marinade with flour mixed with water. Cook until smooth.

Margaret C. Robinson
Pelham, New Hampshire

RIBS WITH HOISIN SAUCE

2-3 lbs. ribs

MARINADE:
1 clove garlic, chopped
2 tbsp. hoisin sauce
2 tbsp. soy sauce
2 tbsp. sherry
2 tbsp. water
Salt and pepper to taste

Mix together marinade ingredients. Coat ribs in mixture, cover, and marinate ribs overnight. Bake in shallow, uncovered pan at 350 degrees for 1 hour.

Richard Beardsley
Boulder, Colorado

HERBED RIB ROAST

6-8 lb. rib roast
¼ cup chopped fresh parsley
1 tsp. dried basil leaves
1 tsp. celery seed
1 tsp. marjoram leaves
1 tsp. dried thyme leaves
1 tsp. salt
¼ tsp. pepper
1 can beef broth (14 oz.)
2 beef bouillon cubes

Preheat oven to 325 degrees. Stand roast, fat side up, in large shallow roasting pan. Roast uncovered, 2½ hours. In small bowl, combine parsley, basil, celery seed, marjoram, thyme, salt, and pepper. Brush surface of roast with pan drippings. Pat herb mixture onto roast. Pour beef broth over roast and add 2 bouillon cubes to broth. Return roast to oven and finish cooking until it reaches desired degree of doneness (140 degrees, rare; 160 degrees, medium; 170 degrees, well done). Slice and serve. Serves 12 or more.

Evelyn Upham
Lakewood, Colorado

DAMET ("DON AND MARIE'S ELK TREAT")

2 lbs. ground lean elk
   meat (moose or
   venison are also okay)
2 medium onions, diced
2 large green peppers,
   diced
1 medium jar stuffed,
   green olives (8 oz.),
   drained (save juice)
2 tbsp. capers
³/₄ cup seedless raisins
1 large can tomato
   sauce (15 oz.)
¹/₂ tsp. each of salt, garlic
   powder, celery salt
¹/₄ tsp. each of dry
   oregano, pepper,
   paprika
1 tbsp. Pickapeppa
   sauce*, or more to
   taste
2 tbsp. Worcestershire
   sauce
4 tbsp. olive oil

*Pickapeppa sauce is a
   delightful additive
   from the island of
   Jamaica. Heinz 57
   or A-1 may be
   substituted.

Sauté onions and peppers in 2 tbsp. olive oil. Remove to side. Sauté meat in 2 tbsp. olive oil; stir in seasonings; add Pickapeppa and Worcestershire sauces, half of juice drained from olives, and tomato sauce; and stir well. Add sautéed onions and peppers and rest of ingredients. Cook, covered, about 40 minutes over slow heat. Serve with, or over, cooked white, wild, or yellow rice. Serves 6-8.

Don Armstrong
Canon City, Colorado

NACHO CASSEROLE

1 lb. ground meat
1 cup chunky salsa
1 cup canned corn
³/₄ cup mayonnaise
1 tbsp. chili powder
2 cups crushed tortilla
   chips
2 cups shredded colby or
   Monterey jack cheese
Lettuce and tomato

Heat oven to 350 degrees. Brown meat in small amount of oil. Drain off oil. Stir in salsa, corn, mayonnaise, and chili powder. Place half of meat in bottom of 2-quart casserole, top with half of chips and then half of cheese. Repeat layers. Bake 20 minutes. Top with additional grated cheese, shredded lettuce, and chopped tomato. Serves 6.

Jan Anderson
Portland, Oregon

ELK CHILI

2 lbs. ground elk
1 lb. smoked sausage,
   chopped
1 onion, diced
6 cloves garlic, crushed
   or minced
3 tbsp. oil
1 pkg. dry chili mix
2 cups water
1 small bottle ketchup
   (15 oz.)
1 can green chilies,
   chopped (7 oz.)
1 can: pinto beans,
   kidney beans, and
   cut green beans
   (10¹/₂ oz. each)
Cayenne pepper

Brown meats, onion, and garlic in oil. Drain. Add chili mix and water and simmer 10 minutes. Add remaining ingredients and simmer 1¹/₂-2 hours, covered, stirring occasionally. To avoid sticking, add water as needed. Add cayenne pepper to taste. Serve over rice with grated cheese. Serves 15-20, depending on appetite.

Betty Warren
Yakima, Washington

Tom's Spicy "Hot" Elk Chili

2 lbs. ground elk
1 medium onion, diced
2 cups beer (or water)
1 oz. unsweetened
  chocolate, cut into
  chunks
3 tbsp. chili powder
1 tbsp. garlic powder
1 ½ tsp. paprika
1 tsp. red pepper flakes
1 tbsp. Accent
1 tbsp. cumin
1 tbsp. white pepper
1 can red or kidney
  beans (16 oz.)

Brown elk with diced onions in small amount of oil. Drain. Add 1 cup beer (or water), the chocolate, and all spices. Heat to melt chocolate. Add remaining beer (or water) and beans. Cover and cook on low heat for 1 hour or more. For best flavor, allow to cool, store in refrigerator overnight and reheat the next day. Sprinkle shredded cheeses on top of chili and serve with hot biscuits. Serves 8 or so.

Tom Dreier
Oshkosh, Wisconsin

Rocky Mountain Elk Firehouse Chili (1989 Arizona State Fair Blue Ribbon Winner)

1 1/2 lbs. ground elk meat

1 large yellow onion, diced

2 cloves garlic, chopped

2 cans tomato sauce (10 1/2 oz. each)

2 cans Italian style stewed tomatoes (15 1/2 oz. each)

1 can dark red kidney beans, drained (15 1/2 oz.)

1 small can diced green chilies

2 fresh jalapeño peppers, diced

2 fresh yellow hot peppers, diced (optional)

1/2 cup red bell pepper, diced

5 tsp. red chili powder

1 1/2 tsp. dry cumin powder

1 tsp. salt

1 tsp. dry oregano

1 tsp. black pepper

1/2 cup brown sugar

Brown elk, onion, and garlic in skillet in small amount of oil. Drain. Add other ingredients, cover, and simmer on low for an hour or more. Serve with Mexican-style corn bread. Serves 4-6.

John Pierce
Tucson, Arizona

CHASON'S CHILE

½ lb. dry pinto beans
5 cups canned tomatoes
I green pepper, chopped
I onion, chopped
I tbsp. plus I tsp.
   salad oil
3½ lbs. ground beef
2 cloves garlic, chopped
½ cup fresh parsley,
   chopped
½ cup chili powder
2 tsp. salt
I½ tsp. paprika
I½ tsp. cumin seed

Wash beans and soak in water overnight. Rinse; add new water to cover and cook until tender. Drain. Add tomatoes. Cook 5 minutes. Sauté green pepper and onions in salad oil. Add ground beef and brown. Add garlic and parsley. Simmer 15 minutes. Add chili powder and remaining ingredients. Add beans and tomatoes. Cook covered 1 hour, then ½ hour uncovered. Serves 10.

Pansy Bowen
Missoula, Montana

SHEPHERD PIE

4 medium potatoes,
   peeled
I egg, beaten
½ cup milk
I lb. elk or deer burger
Oil for browning
1-2 cups canned corn,
   drained
I cup shredded cheese
2 cans cream of
   mushroom soup

Boil potatoes until done, drain, add egg and small amount of milk to potatoes. Mash and set aside. Brown burger in small amount of oil, and mix in the corn, cheese, and mushroom soup. When mixed well, place in a casserole dish. Place mashed potatoes on top of mixture, spreading evenly. Place in a 350-degree oven and bake for 35 minutes or until heated through and potatoes are golden brown. Serves 4-5.

Maggie Justice
Selah, Washington

ENCHILADAS

1 cup onions, chopped
1 clove garlic, chopped
1 tbsp. oil
1 lb. elk burger, cooked
1 large can solid packed
   tomatoes (28 oz.)
1 can tomato paste
   (6 oz.)
2 cups water
1 ½ tsp. salt
1 tbsp. Worcestershire
   sauce
1 tbsp. chili powder
Dash Tabasco sauce
Pinch each: oregano,
   cumin seed,
   rosemary, thyme
16 six-inch flour tortillas
8 oz. Monterey jack
   cheese, grated

Sauté onions and garlic in small amount of oil. Drain. Add all ingredients except last two. Cover and simmer for awhile. Add more water if needed. Grease 9 x 14-inch baking dish. Put small amount of sauce on bottom of pan. With slotted spoon, remove meat mixture from sauce and fill tortillas. Roll them. Place in baking dish side by side, seam side down. Cover with remaining sauce and sprinkle with the cheese. Cover with foil and bake at 350 degrees for 30 minutes. Serves 4-8.

Yvonne Decker
Libby, Montana

Taco Lasagna

1 lb. ground lean
  antelope, elk, moose,
  or deer meat
1 large onion, chopped
1 jar spaghetti sauce
  (12-16 oz.)
3 large corn tortillas
1 can cream style corn
  (8 oz.)
Grated mozzarella and
  cheddar cheese,
  8 oz. each, mixed

Sauté onions in very small amount of vegetable oil. Add meat and brown. Add spaghetti sauce. Lightly oil a casserole dish that fits the tortillas. Place a tortilla on the bottom, add a layer of meat mix, a layer of corn, and a layer of cheese mix. Build up two additional similar layers (3 layers total). Bake about 20 minutes or until hot and cheese is melted. Serves 3 or 4.

Don Armstrong
Canon City, Colorado

J Venison Casserole

Corn tortillas,
  cut in strips
Grated cheddar cheese

Meat Filling:
1½ lb. ground venison
2 tbsp. salad oil
1 green pepper, chopped
1 onion, chopped
1 can tomatoes
  (14½ oz.)
1 tsp. chili powder
1 tsp. cumin
1 tsp. dried oregano
2 cans cream of
  mushroom soup
  (10¾ oz.)
1 cup beef broth

Sauté venison in oil, add green pepper and onion and sauté briefly. Add remaining meat filling ingredients and heat through. In large baking dish (9 x 13-inch) start with one layer of strips of corn tortillas; add a layer of meat filling and light layer of grated cheddar cheese; repeat layers (several layers) and cover the last layer with grated cheddar cheese. Cover with foil and bake at 350 degrees for 30-35 minutes. Freezes well. Serves 6-8.

Ann W. Olson
Houston, Texas

Derevi Dolma with Elk
(Grape leaves stuffed with ground elk)

STUFFING:

1 lb. ground elk

2 small or medium-sized
onions, chopped fine

1 clove garlic, crushed

1/2 cup tomatoes, canned
and drained or fresh,
chopped

1/2 cup instant rice

1 tbsp. soft margarine

1 tbsp. chopped, fresh
parsley

5 or 6 fresh mint leaves,
chopped fine

Salt and pepper to taste

Fresh or canned grape
leaves

BRAISING SAUCE:

Juice from 1/2 lemon

2 cans beef broth
(about 10 oz. each)

Mix all the stuffing ingredients
except the grape leaves. Cut the stems
from the grape leaves and soak them in
boiling water if they are fresh, or wash
them in hot water if they are canned.
Drain and place one layer of leaves in
bottom of a baking dish. Then take 2 of
the remaining leaves and place wrong
side up on a flat surface with the stem
end towards you. Put 2 spoonfuls of
meat mix near stem end, fold the sides
of the leaf in over the meat and roll
from the stem end. Continue with
remaining leaves and place all the rolls
side by side in the baking dish. Mix
braising sauce and pour into baking
dish. Sauce should just cover leaves.
Cover dish and bake in a preheated oven
for 1 hour at 350 degrees. These can be
served hot for a main dish or hot or cold
as appetizers. Makes 3-5 dozen
depending on size of grape leaves.

Ted Martin
Clovis, California

BISCUIT-TOPPED ITALIAN VENISON CASSEROLE

1 lb. ground venison
¹/₂ cup chopped onion
Oil for browning
³/₄ cup water
¹/₄ tsp. black pepper
**1 can tomato sauce
   (8 oz.)**
**1 can tomato paste
   (6 oz.)**
Dash of salt
Dash of garlic powder
**1 pkg. frozen mixed
   vegetables, thawed
   and drained (16 oz.)**
**8 oz. (2 cups) shredded
   mozzarella cheese**
**1 can refrigerated
   buttermilk biscuits
   (10 oz.)**
**¹/₂ tsp. dried oregano
   leaves, crushed, or
   use parsley flakes**

Heat oven to 375 degrees. Grease 12 x 8-inch (2 qt.) baking dish. In large skillet, brown ground venison and onion in small amount of oil. Drain. Stir in water, pepper, salt, garlic, tomato sauce, and tomato paste; simmer for 15 minutes, stirring occasionally. Remove from heat; stir in vegetables and 1¹/₂ cups of the cheese. Spoon mixture into greased baking dish. Separate dough into 10 biscuits. Separate each biscuit into 2 layers. Place biscuits near outer edge of hot meat mixture, overlapping slightly. Sprinkle remaining cheese in center and around edge. Gently brush biscuits with margarine; sprinkle with oregano. Bake at 375 degrees for 25-30 minutes or until biscuits are golden brown. Serves 6-8.

Ann W. Olson
Houston, Texas

VENISON CHEESEBURGER PIE

1 cup plus 2 tbsp. biscuit
   baking mix
1/2 cup water
1 lb. ground venison
2 tsp. minced onion
1/2 tsp. salt
1/4 tsp. pepper
1 tbsp. Worcestershire
   sauce
2 eggs
1 cup small curd cottage
   cheese
2 medium tomatoes,
   sliced
1 cup shredded cheddar
   cheese

Preheat oven to 375 degrees. Mix one cup baking mix and water to form soft dough, beat vigorously for 20 strokes. Gently smooth dough into ball. Roll out dough on flour-covered board 2 inches larger than inverted 9-inch pie pan. Place dough in pan. Flute edges. Set aside. Cook venison and onions in small amount of oil until brown. Drain. Stir in salt, pepper, 2 tbsp. baking mix, and Worcestershire sauce. Spoon mix into pie crust. Mix eggs and cottage cheese and pour over venison mixture. Arrange tomato slices on top and sprinkle with cheddar cheese. Bake until set, about 30 minutes. Serves 6.

VARIATION: Beverly Hyde of Post Falls, Idaho uses an unbaked pastry shell instead of making one from biscuits. She also adds chopped green pepper and salsa to the meat mixture.

Alice Taylor
Eagle, Idaho

ELK PIE

1 lb. ground elk
2 tbsp. butter or
  margarine
1 garlic clove, minced
1 medium onion,
  chopped
1 envelope onion soup
  mix
2 cups red or rosé wine
1 cup water
1 tbsp. Mrs. Dash
1 tsp. fresh parsley,
  chopped
$1/4$ tsp. dried rosemary
$1/4$ tsp dried basil
$1/2$ lb. fresh mushrooms,
  chopped
1 cup sliced carrots
1 cup frozen peas
2 tbsp. flour
$1/4$ cup water
2 double pie crusts

Brown elk meat in butter or margarine with the garlic and onion until brown. Add onion soup mix, wine, water, and seasonings. Bring to boil and add mushrooms and carrots. Cook on medium heat for 15 minutes; add frozen peas and cook 5 minutes. Thicken with flour mixed with water. Pour into 2 pie shells and cover with pie crust. Provide steam slits and bake at 425 degrees for about 15 minutes until browned. Serve immediately. Serves 6-8.

Margaret C. Robinson
Pelham, New Hampshire

ELK MEATBALLS

1 lb. elk burger
1 large onion, finely
  chopped
1 tsp. salt
$^1/_2$ tsp. black pepper
1 grated apple
$^1/_2$ cup bread crumbs

GRAVY:

2 cups water
1 tsp. paprika
4 tbsp. flour

Mix first 6 ingredients together, form balls (golf ball size). Place in 9 x 13-inch pan, cover with gravy. Cook 1 hour at 350 degrees, uncovered. Makes 10-12 meatballs.

Necia Knudson
Heart K Ranch, Washington

ELK BALLS

2 lbs. ground elk
1 pkg. dry onion soup mix
2 eggs
$^1/_2$ cup rolled oats,
  uncooked
Salt and pepper to taste
$^1/_2$ tsp. garlic powder
$^1/_4$ cup milk

SAUCE:

1 jar chili sauce (12 oz.)
1 jar grape jelly (12 oz.)

Mix first 7 ingredients. Form into balls and put on cookie sheet. Bake 15-30 minutes, depending on size of meatballs, at 350 degrees. Mix jelly and chili sauce together. Put cooked meatballs into baking dish or crock pot. Pour sauce over meatballs. Bake until heated thoroughly. Makes about 30 meatballs.

Sandy Rabe

BARBECUE MEATBALLS

I lb. hamburger
¹/₂ cup milk
¹/₂ tsp. salt
³/₄ cup rolled oats,
   uncooked
¹/₂ chopped onion

SAUCE:
I cup ketchup
¹/₂ cup water
¹/₂ chopped onion
2 tbsp. vinegar
4 tbsp. brown sugar

Mix first 5 ingredients well and form into 1-inch balls. Place in a 13 x 9- inch baking dish. Mix sauce ingredients and pour over raw meatballs. Do not cover. Bake at 350 degrees for 1 hour, turning twice during baking. Makes about 24 meatballs.

Patty Bogh
McMinnville, Oregon

Elk Burgers

1 lb. ground elk
2 medium onions, diced
1 green pepper, diced
1 tbsp. Worcestershire
   sauce
1/8 tsp. garlic powder
1/8 tsp. salt
1/8 tsp. black pepper
1 egg
1/2 cup flour

Mix ingredients and shape into patties. Broil until done and serve on rolls with sliced tomato, lettuce, and mayonnaise. Serves 4.

Dianne J. Sage
Livingston, Montana

Wapiti Burgers for the Grill

Elk burger
Chopped onion
Chopped green pepper
Chopped mushrooms
Shredded cheese
   (optional)

Make an even number of 1/2-inch patties and set aside in a cool place. Chop onion, green pepper, and mushrooms. Place the patties in pairs, and put the vegetable mixture on top of half of them, adding shredded cheese if you like cheeseburgers. Put the remaining patties on top and press them together, being sure to pinch the edges together to avoid a blowout on the grill. Barbecue until done, and season to taste.

Rick Anzalone
Chehalis, Washington

Marinated Venison Burgers

1 1/2 lbs. ground venison,
   made into 6 patties
1 cup dry white wine
1 chopped green onion
1 tsp. beef bouillon
   granules
1 tsp. Worcestershire
   sauce
1/2 tsp. salt
1/8 tsp. pepper
6 hamburger buns
   (or sourdough rolls)
   split, buttered, and
   toasted

In shallow baking dish mix wine, onion, bouillon, Worcestershire sauce, and seasonings until granules are dissolved. Place venison patties in marinade. Refrigerate 2-3 hours, turning several times. Drain patties and reserve marinade. Place meat on broiler pan 3-5 inches from heat and broil for 5-7 minutes. Turn and broil an additional 5-7 minutes. Brush with marinade once or twice during broiling. Makes 6.

Robert and Michele Sandness
LaMoure, North Dakota

Elk Gyro Burgers

1 lb. ground elk
1 lb. ground lamb
1 egg
¹/₄ cup water
¹/₂ cup bread crumbs
¹/₄ tsp. garlic powder
¹/₄ tsp. cinnamon
¹/₄ tsp. allspice
¹/₄ tsp. dried thyme
¹/₂ tsp. dried sweet basil
2 tsp. dried oregano
1 tbsp. sugar

Yogurt Sauce:
2 tsp. dried parsley flakes
1/4 cup onions, diced
1/4 cup cucumbers, diced
1 cup yogurt, plain
5 tbsp. sour cream
1 tbsp. sugar

Combine first 12 ingredients. Mix well. Cover and chill overnight. Combine ingredients for sauce. Cover and chill overnight. Shape meat into 8 patties. Grill until entirely cooked. Serve on pita bread or homemade buns with lettuce, sliced tomatoes, onions, and yogurt sauce on top. A dash of cayenne pepper is great!

Debora Ann Petty
Columbia Falls, Montana

MEAT LOAF

¹/₂ c. **Grape Nuts cereal**
¹/₂ **cup milk**
I can tomato sauce
  (8 oz.)
2 lbs. venison, ground
¹/₂ **cup grated onion**
I ¹/₂ **tsp. salt**
2 eggs
¹/₂ **tsp. dried oregano**

SAUCE FOR TOP:
8 oz. tomato sauce
I tbsp. vinegar
6 tbsp. water
I tbsp. prepared
  mustard
4 tbsp. brown sugar

Combine cereal, milk, and 8 oz. tomato sauce with venison and onion. Add eggs, oregano, and salt. Mix well. Put meat in 9 x 5-inch loaf pan and bake at 350 degrees for 1 hour. Mix sauce ingredients and heat. Pour over meat loaf before serving. Serves 6.

Jolene Kennedy
Shawnee Mission, Kansas

WAPITI MOUNTAIN MEAT LOAF

2 lbs. elk or venison
   burger
1 small onion, chopped
$^1/_4$ cup green pepper,
   chopped
1 egg
$^1/_4$ cup milk
$^1/_2$-$^3/_4$ cup cracker
   crumbs
1 can tomato sauce
   (8 oz.)
Salt, pepper, garlic
   powder, oregano to
   taste
2 tbsp. mustard seed

Mix all ingredients, saving half of the tomato sauce. Put in 9 x 5-inch loaf pan. Spread remaining tomato sauce on top. Bake 1-1$^1/_2$ hours in 350 degree oven.

OPTIONAL: Line bottom of pan with bacon which adds taste and prevents sticking. Serves 6.

Doug Roffers
Shawano, Wisconsin

ELK "I THINK I PUT EVERYTHING IN" MEAT LOAF

2¹/₂ lb. elk burger
¹/₃ lb. pork sausage
2 onion burger buns,
   broken up
2 eggs
I onion, chopped
¹/₂ green pepper,
   chopped
¹/₄ cup canned whole
   kernel corn
¹/₂ stalk celery, chopped
I tsp. pepper
I tsp. salt
I tsp. fennel seed,
   crushed
I tsp. dried basil
I tsp. crushed, dried
   rosemary
I tbsp. dried oregano
I tbsp. Parmesan cheese
¹/₂ cup milk
¹/₂ cup red wine
3 medium red potatoes,
   sliced
I can mushroom soup
   (10³/₄ oz.)

Beat eggs thoroughly in a bowl. In a large mixing bowl add the egg and onion buns to the meat and mix with your own eager mitts. Add the remaining ingredients except the red wine and mushroom soup, and mix thoroughly again. Form the meat mixture in the shape of your cooking dish or small roasting pan. Place meat in floured dish or pan. Mix the red wine and mushroom soup and pour over the meat loaf. Place in 350-degree oven for 50 minutes, or until done. Serves 12.

James E. Pinch
Bellevue, Washington

APPLE-CHEESE LOAF

¹/₂ cup apple butter

I tsp. salt

¹/₄ tsp. ground nutmeg

¹/₈ tsp. pepper

I ¹/₂ lbs. ground beef or lamb

I cup dried coarse bread crumbs

I small onion, finely chopped

I egg

4 oz. cheddar cheese, cut into ¹/₂-inch cubes

Preheat oven to 325 degrees. Combine apple butter, salt, nutmeg, and pepper. Add meat, bread crumbs, onions, and egg. Mix lightly but thoroughly with hands. Fold in cheese cubes. Mold into a loaf. Bake in a shallow pan or loaf pan for 1 hour. Also great for meatloaf sandwiches! Serves 6.

Sally Gregory
Lemhi, Idaho

COTTONTAIL CASSEROLE

**I rabbit, dressed and
    disjointed**
Salted water
Flour
8 slices of bacon
2 medium onions, sliced
**2 medium potatoes,
    sliced**
I tsp. salt
¹/₄ tsp. pepper

Let the disjointed rabbit stand in salted water for 1 hour. Then remove, wipe dry, and roll in flour. Fry the bacon in skillet until light brown. Remove the bacon and fry the rabbit in the bacon fat until golden brown. Arrange the meat in a casserole and place over it the sliced onions, potatoes, and bacon. Dust all lightly with flour, add salt and pepper, and pour hot water over to cover. Cover and bake 2 hours in a 350-degree oven. Serves 4.

F. Dale Foley
Winlock, Washington

CAJUN SIX-PACK
SQUIRREL JAMBALAYA

6 squirrels, cleaned (can substitute chicken, rabbits, or other small game)
8 onions, chopped
Tabasco sauce to taste
Salt, pepper (black and cayenne) to taste
$1/2$ cup Creole seasoning
4 lbs. smoked sausage, cut in $1/4$-inch pieces
$1/2$ lb. pork, cubed
4 garlic cloves, chopped fine
2 bunches celery, chopped
2 bunches shallots, chopped fine
8 cups squirrel stock
2 bay leaves
4 cups white rice
2-4 tbsp. Worcestershire sauce
I six-pack beer (optional)

Boil squirrels, covered, in water seasoned with 2 chopped onions, salt, pepper, $1/4$ cup Creole seasoning, and anything else you want to put in, until tender. Remove meat, bone, and put in refrigerator to cool. Save stock. Drink one beer. Fry sausage and drain off grease. Put aside. Save some grease to brown pork cubes. Set browned pork aside. Drink one beer. In pork grease, sauté garlic, onions, celery, and shallots until soft. Add stock and bay leaves. Bring to boil. Drink one beer. Add all meat. Bring back to boil. Add remaining Creole seasoning and rice. Mix well. Bring to boil, turn heat very low. Cover and keep lid on for 30 minutes. When rice is tender, add 2-4 tbsp. Worcestershire sauce and up to 4 tsp. of Tabasco, to taste. Drink remaining beer. You deserve it. Feeds 6 Cajuns or 10 others.

Stufato di Cervo al Vino Rosso

MARINADE INGREDIENTS:

3 cups dry red wine
1 cup dry madeira
4-5 garlic cloves, minced
3 bay leaves
2 tsp. dried thyme
1 tsp. coarse cracked
   lemon pepper
10 juniper berries,
   crushed

STEW INGREDIENTS:

2-3 lbs. elk hind quarter,
   cut in 1-1½-inch
   pieces (cut off silver
   skin and fat)
4 oz. top-quality bacon,
   diced
2 medium onions,
   chopped
2-3 cups sliced
   mushrooms
1 tbsp. butter
1 tbsp. olive oil
   (if needed)
3 tbsp. flour
1 cup elk or beef stock
2 large potatoes, peeled
   and cut in 2-inch
   cubes
2 tbsp. red or black
   currant jelly
2 tbsp. Worcestershire
   sauce
1 tsp. freshly ground
   black pepper
2 tbsp. soy sauce
1 tbsp. tomato paste
1 tsp. salt
Sour cream (optional)

Stufato di Cervo (cont.)

Combine all marinade ingredients in a large bowl. Add elk cubes
and mix well. Cover and marinate 2 hours at room temperature. In a
large stewpot, fry the bacon until crisp. Remove and drain. Add
onions to bacon fat and sauté until browned. Remove onions, drain.
Save bacon fat. In separate skillet, sauté mushrooms in the butter and
set aside. After the meat has marinated, remove the elk pieces with a
slotted spoon. Reserve the liquid. Dry the elk with paper towels and
brown a few pieces at a time on all sides in bacon fat over medium
heat. Add an additional tbsp. olive oil if necessary to brown meat.
Return all meat and accumulated juices to stewpot and sprinkle with
the flour. Stir well and cook about 3-4 minutes or until flour is
browned.

Strain marinade and add it to the pot. Stir in the rest of the
ingredients (except the mushrooms, onions, bacon, and sour cream).
Cook uncovered over low heat (maintain a good simmer) for 1 hour,
stirring occasionally. Sauce should thicken nicely. Add the onions and
cook another hour. Add the mushrooms and crisp bacon and heat
another 15 minutes. When serving, put a dollop of sour cream in the
center of each portion. Serve with French bread, fresh garden salad,
and any good red wine. The following Italian wines are a few of my
favorites: Renato Ratti Barolo, Bruno Giacosa Barbaresco, or
Fontanafredda Barolo. Serves 4-6.

Edgar S. Burks, Jr.
Shreveport, Louisiana

VENISON AND MUSHROOM STEW

8 tbsp. butter or
margarine (1 stick)
2 lbs. venison
(or antelope), cut
into 1-inch chunks
5 tbsp. flour
2 tsp. paprika
1 1/2 tsp. ground
coriander
Salt and pepper
3 cups seeded and diced
plum tomatoes
2 cups chicken broth
1 1/2 cups yellow onions,
cut in slivers
6 whole shallots, peeled
and chopped
2 cloves garlic, peeled
and minced
1/4 cup chopped parsley
1 tbsp. dried tarragon
Grated zest of one
orange
1/2 lb. fresh mushrooms,
halved
1/2 cup heavy cream

Preheat oven to 350 degrees. Melt 4 tbsp. butter in a heavy casserole. Add venison and brown. Mix 2 tbsp. flour, paprika, coriander, salt, and pepper. Sprinkle over venison and cook over low heat, stirring, for 5 minutes.

Add 2 cups tomatoes, chicken broth, onions, shallots, garlic, parsley, tarragon, and orange zest. Bring to a boil. Cover and bake in oven for 1 1/4 hours at 350 degrees. Sauté mushrooms in 1 tbsp. butter until golden. Reserve. Remove stew from oven and strain. Set aside stew meat and stew liquid. Put casserole on stove and melt 3 tbsp. butter. Add 3 tbsp. flour and cook, whisking, for 2 minutes. Slowly whisk in stew liquid, stir for 5 minutes. Whisk in cream. Add stew meat, remaining tomatoes, and mushrooms and heat for 5 minutes. Serve over rice or noodles. Serves 6.

Shelley Gilligan
Hillsborough, California

Venison Stew

½ lb. bacon
2 lbs. venison, cut into
   small chunks
¼ cup flour
1 pkg. frozen peas
1 can crushed tomatoes
   (16 oz.)
2 cans beer
Onions (to taste),
   chopped
Carrots (to taste),
   chopped
Celery (to taste),
   chopped
Turnips (to taste),
   chopped
2 bouillon cubes
1 tbsp. sugar
½ tsp. dried thyme
¼ tsp. black pepper
⅛ tsp. red pepper

Cook bacon until crispy. Remove from pan. In bacon drippings, brown floured venison. Add all ingredients except bacon and simmer until vegetables are tender. Crumble bacon on top of stew and cook 10 minutes more.

Ed Gran
New Kent, Virginia

MIKE'S WHITE RIVER STEW

1-1½ lbs. elk stew meat

**1-1½ lbs. venison stew
  meat**

**1¼ cups whole wheat
  flour**

1 tbsp. garlic powder

1 tbsp. salt

**1 tbsp. Lawry's seasoned
  pepper**

2½ tbsp. butter

2½ tbsp. margarine

**2 large peeled and diced
  white onions**

7 cups hot water

6 whole bay leaves

**¼ cup dried parsley
  flakes**

**6-8 peeled and cut
  carrots**

**6-8 unpeeled, medium
  to large, cut potatoes**

Trim all bone, fat, and waste from the meat. Set aside ½ cup of the flour for use later. In a bowl, combine the remaining flour with the garlic powder, salt, and seasoned pepper. Dredge the meat, 1 piece at a time, through the flour mixture and set aside. Melt the butter and margarine in a Dutch oven. Add the onions and sauté. Add the meat and lightly brown. Drain off fat. Add the hot water, bay leaves, parsley flakes, carrots, and potatoes. Bring to a boil, stirring occasionally. Shake the ½ cup flour set aside earlier with some water and add to pot, mixing. Reduce heat and cover. Let simmer 4-6 hours. Serves 8-12.

Create Mike's "Raging" White River Stew by adding ⅓-½ cup Jack Daniels whiskey with the hot water.

*Michael J. Dafni
Lakewood, Colorado*

BUCKHORN CAMP VENISON AND MUSHROOM STEW

3-4 lbs. lean venison, cut in bite-sized pieces
2-3 lbs. mushrooms, medium size
6-8 cans beef broth (10 oz. each)
4 or 5 large onions, sliced
I lb. butter or margarine
3 cups flour
Burgundy wine
3-4 bay leaves
2 tsp. thyme, ground
Lots of fresh ground pepper
I pkg. flat noodles (12 oz.), cooked

Heat up a large cast iron Dutch oven and melt down half of the butter. Put the flour in a bag and dredge half the venison. Brown the venison and keep scraping the bottom of the pan. Remove the meat and repeat with the other half of the butter and venison. With all the meat in the pan add the onions, half of the beef broth, all of the spices, and about four "glugs" of the wine. Simmer over low heat, stirring occasionally until venison is tender. Add more beef broth if needed. Set the Dutch oven aside in refrigerator until about dinner time, then reheat. Add more beef broth, throw in the mushrooms, a couple more "glugs" of wine (to taste) and cook until the mushrooms are just hot. Put a good-sized heap of the noodles in a shallow bowl and ladle the stew on top. Have bread handy to mop up the gravy. Serves 10-12.

Frank P. Conger
Redmond, Washington

ELKIN STEW

2 lbs. fat-free elk meat, cut into 1-inch cubes
Cooking oil
1 medium onion, diced
4 cups water
1½ tbsp. chili powder
1 tsp. salt
1 tsp. garlic powder
4 cups raw pumpkin, peeled and cubed
1 can yellow corn (10 oz.)
2 tbsp. flour

In a Dutch oven, brown meat in oil. Remove meat and sauté onion in drippings. Add a little more oil if needed. Cook onion until half done. Return meat to Dutch oven, add 4 cups water. Simmer, covered, for 1½ hours. Add pumpkin, corn, salt, chili powder, and garlic powder. Simmer, covered, for 45 minutes. Mix flour with ¼ cup water, stir into stew, and cook until thickened. Serves 6.

Jim Dunford
Fort Jones, California

RED STEW

1 ½ lbs. elk or venison,
   cut in small pieces
Oil for browning
2-3 cups carrots, sliced
2 onions, sliced
2 cloves garlic, chopped
1 ½ tbsp. chili powder
1 tbsp. sugar
Salt and pepper to taste
1-2 cans tomato sauce
   (8 oz. each)
½ lb. sharp cheese,
   grated

Brown meat in small amount of oil. Add sliced carrots, onions, and garlic towards end of browning, stirring frequently until cooked. Add tomato sauce, chili powder, sugar, salt, and pepper. Let simmer until all is tender. Top with grated cheese and serve. Serves 4-6.

Barbara J. Nelson
Salinas, California

MOOSE SIMMERED IN BEER

2 lbs. lean moose cubes
2 tbsp. flour
¼ tsp. fines herbes
½ tsp. sodium glutamate
Salt and pepper to taste
2 cups minced onion
1 tbsp. bacon fat
1 bay leaf
1 bottle of beer (12 oz.)

Mix flour, herbs, sodium glutamate, salt, and pepper in a bag. Add meat cubes and shake well. Heat fat, add onions. Fry on slow fire until golden brown. Add meat and brown. Pour beer over the meat, add bay leaf, cover and simmer for 2 hours. At end of cooking time, if there is too much liquid, thicken with 1 tbsp. browned flour mixed with a little water. Cook thoroughly. Serves 6-8.

F. Dale Foley
Winlock, Washington

Laura's BBQ Meat and Beans

2 lbs. wild game stew
  meat
2 cans stewed tomatoes
  (14½ oz. each)
2 cans premium baked
  beans (16 oz. each)
1 large onion, chopped
2 tbsp. prepared
  mustard
2 tbsp. salsa
½ cup barbecue sauce

Combine all ingredients in a large covered casserole dish. Bake at 325 degrees for 3 hours. Also good cooked in a Dutch oven or slow cooker. Serves 5-6 or 4 hungry hunters.

Laura Nelson
Smithfield, Utah

Venison or Elk Stroganoff

1 lb. meat (venison or
  elk) cut in bite-size
  pieces
½ cup flour
1 tsp. salt
⅛ tsp. pepper
2 tbsp. oil
1 onion, chopped
1 clove garlic, minced
1 can mushrooms (4 oz.)
  (fresh are better)
1 cube beef bouillon
  dissolved in 1 cup
  water (consommé)
1 tbsp. Worcestershire
  sauce
½ cup green pepper,
  chopped
1 cup sour cream

Combine flour, salt, and pepper in a bag. Toss meat to coat. Brown meat in oil. Add onion, garlic, and mushrooms. Sauté until partially tender. Add consommé, Worcestershire sauce, and green peppers. Bring to a boil, then simmer until tender, approximately 1 hour. Add 1 cup sour cream just before serving. Heat through and serve over buttered noodles. Makes 4 servings.

Sharon Kilmer
Arlington, Washington

ELK OR DEER MEAT STROGANOFF

2 lbs. elk or deer meat,
 cubed
Salt
Pepper
Meat tenderizer
$^1/_2$ cup flour
3 tbsp. olive oil
$^3/_4$ cup burgundy wine
 (or non-alcoholic
 wine)
1 cup beef bouillon or
 broth
$^1/_2$-1 cup non-fat sour
 cream
3 green onions, chopped
Brown rice for 4-6
 people

Sprinkle meat with salt, pepper, and meat tenderizer, and coat with flour. Brown in large frying pan in hot oil. Turn once until nicely browned. Add wine and bouillon and let simmer 30 minutes or until done. Add sour cream. Simmer until sour cream is mixed and hot. Top with green onions and serve over rice. Serves 4-6.

NOTE: You can also add 10-12 sliced fresh mushrooms and simmer 5-10 minutes before adding sour cream.

Jann Weber

CREOLE ELK WITH RICE

**1 lb. elk round steak,
sliced paper thin**
1 cup celery, diced
**1 cup green pepper,
diced**
1 cup onions, diced
**1 can mushrooms,
drained (8 oz.)**
1 cup Burgundy wine
**Creole seasoning
to taste**
White rice for 4 people

CREOLE SEASONING:
**26 oz. box free flowing
salt**
**1 1/2 oz. box ground
black pepper**
**2 oz. bottle ground red
pepper**
**1 oz. bottle garlic
powder**
1 oz. bottle chili powder

Mix Creole seasoning ingredients well. Use like salt. Store in airtight container. Makes enough for several meals.

Brown elk steak in small amount of oil. Remove steak and add celery, green peppers, and onion. Sauté until just tender. Put steak back in pan with wine, mushrooms, and Creole seasoning. Heat through. May have to thicken with cornstarch mixed with a small amount of water. Serve over white rice. Serves 4.

Dianne J. Sage
Livingston, Montana

SHERIDA'S ITALIAN ELK CASSEROLE

2 lbs. elk or deer, cut in small pieces

1 large onion, chopped

1 bell pepper, chopped

Oil for sautéing

2 eggs

1/2 cup milk

Prepared Italian bread crumbs

3 cans stewed tomatoes (14 1/2 oz. each)

1 can tomato sauce (8 oz.)

1 can tomato paste (6 oz.)

1-2 cups Provolone cheese, grated

Sauté onion and peppers in oil for a few minutes until just tender. Remove from pan. Mix eggs and milk. Dip elk in milk and then roll in bread crumbs. Add more oil to pan if needed and brown meat. Remove from pan, put elk in 9 x 13-inch baking dish. Mix tomatoes, tomato paste, and tomato sauce and pour over meat. Add onions and green peppers. Cover with foil, bake slowly for several hours. When ready to serve, remove foil and sprinkle with cheese. Bake for 5 minutes at 350 degrees until cheese is melted. Serve with rice. Serves 6-8.

Sherida K. Galley
Willow Park, Texas

Delicious Venison or Elk Stew

1¹/₂-2 lbs. elk, cut into
  ¹/₂-inch bite-sized
  pieces
Buttermilk for marinade
³/₄ cup diced celery
³/₄ cup diced onion
6 carrots, cut up
3-4 potatoes w/skins,
  cut into quarters
1 can stewed tomatoes
  (14¹/₂ oz.)
2 cups water
1 slice bread, broken up
3¹/₂ tbsp. quick cooking
  tapioca
1 tbsp. sugar
1-2 tsp. salt and pepper
  to taste

Marinate elk pieces in buttermilk 2 hours or more. Drain off marinade and put stew meat (not browned) and vegetables, except tomatoes, in large Dutch oven. Sprinkle tapioca on top, add bread, stewed tomatoes, and water last. Bake covered at 325 degrees for 3¹/₂ hours or until gravy thickens. Serve with biscuits and honey. Delicious and very low fat! Serves 6-8.

Barbara Brown
Golden, Colorado

perhaps for hunting trip with rice!

Easy Crockpot Elk

1 medium onion,
    chopped
Flour
1/2 lb. fresh mushrooms,
    sliced
Margarine
1-2 lbs. elk steak, cut in
    serving pieces
1-2 cans stewed
    tomatoes
    (14 1/2 oz. each)
Garlic salt
Onion salt
Pepper

In a fry pan, brown chopped onions and sliced mushrooms in melted margarine. Shake elk steak pieces in flour and lay on browned onions and mushrooms. Brown the meat, and salt and pepper each side of the meat to suit your taste. Add some water and simmer steaks for 3-5 minutes, forming a gravy mixture. Put 1 can of stewed tomatoes in the electric slow-cooking pot. Remove steaks and gravy mixture from your fry pan and layer into the pot. Pour another can of tomatoes on top. Use about 1 can of tomatoes per one pound of meat. The meat and gravy mixture should be about even in your pot. Heat in the pot on a medium setting for 6-8 hours. Serve with mashed potatoes or rice. The meat is tender and tasty, and you will get compliments from the hunters!

NOTE: For variation on Crockpot Elk see Paulette Nelson's Elk Burgundy which follows.

Sharon Read
Kalispell, Montana

ELK BURGUNDY

1½-2 lbs. elk meat,
   cubed
1 bouillon cube (beef)
1 cup cream of
   mushroom soup
1 pkg. dry onion soup
   mix
1 can mushrooms (6 oz.)
½ cup water
1 cup red wine

Put meat in crockpot and add rest of ingredients. Cook 6 to 8 hours on low. Serve over rice or noodles. Serves 4-6.

Paulette Nelson
Mesa, Arizona

VENISON IN WINE

3 lbs. venison, cut in
   1-inch cubes
2 bay leaves
1 can cream of
   mushroom soup
   (10¾ oz.)
1 can French onion soup
   (10¾ oz.)
¾ cup dry red wine
8 oz. sliced mushrooms
¼ cup brandy
1 small onion, chopped
   and sautéed

Place all ingredients except brandy in large casserole. Cover and bake at 350 degrees for 3½ hours or until tender. Add brandy and cook 30 minutes longer. Serve over mashed potatoes or noodles. Serves 6.

Anna Cook
Fort Collins, Colorado

ORIENTAL ELK STROGANOFF

¹/₂ cup soy sauce
¹/₃ cup sherry
1¹/₂ tbsp. fresh ginger, grated
¹/₂ tbsp. sugar
1 clove garlic, crushed
3 lbs. sirloin, cut into chunks (if animal is tender, can use round steak)
3 tbsp. butter or margarine
¹/₂-1 cup chopped onions
1 lb. mushrooms, sliced
1¹/₂ tbsp. flour
Salt and pepper to taste
¹/₂ cup sour cream
2-4 tbsp. fresh snipped parsley

Combine first 5 ingredients and marinate meat in refrigerator for at least 4 hours. Drain and reserve marinade. Sauté onions and mushrooms in margarine, remove from pan, saving liquid. Add a little more margarine and sauté meat in pan for 3 minutes, keeping it on the rare side. Remove from pan and keep warm. Add water to reserved marinade to make 1 cup. Return mushroom liquid to pan and heat. Stir in flour and add the marinade. Cook until thickened. Add beef, onions, mushrooms, salt, pepper, and sour cream. Don't boil, just heat thoroughly. Add parsley and serve over hot noodles. Serves 4-6.

NOTE: Stroganoff can also be made with deer, moose, or duck breasts.

SAUSAGE BRUNCH CASSEROLE

1 lb. lean sausage
12 eggs, beaten
2 cups milk
10 slices bread, torn up
1 cup cheddar cheese,
   shredded

Brown sausage in skillet, stirring until crumbly. Drain. Mix eggs and milk and bread in a bowl. Add half of the cheese and all of the sausage. Mix well. Pour into buttered 9 x 13-inch baking dish. Sprinkle with remaining cheese. Cover with foil and refrigerate overnight. Bake at 350 degrees for 30 minutes or until golden brown. Serves 12.

Sharon Robertson
Kansas City, Kansas

LIVER WITH ONIONS

1 lb. liver
2 onions, sliced
1/2 cup celery, chopped
2 slices ginger root,
   peeled
2 tbsp. peanut oil
1 cup flour

MARINADE:
3 tbsp. oyster sauce
1 tbsp. soy sauce
1 tsp. sesame oil

Cut liver into 1-inch squares. Marinate in oyster sauce mix for 30 minutes. Remove and dredge liver in flour. Heat peanut oil in frying pan or wok until hot. Sauté ginger slices 1 minute. Remove. Add liver. Brown over high heat. Add onion rings and celery. Cover. Simmer 15 minutes, adding small amounts of water as needed to avoid drying out. Serves 4-6.

Richard Beardsley
Boulder, Colorado

Spiced Heart

Heart (elk, deer,
  or moose)
4 cups hot water
¹/₃ cup vinegar
2 tsp. salt
3 tbsp. sugar
3 bay leaves
18 whole cloves
³/₄ cup sliced onion
1 tbsp. grated lemon rind

Place all ingredients in a slow cooker and cook until tender, about 12 hours. Slice and serve either hot or cold.

Suzette Horton
Idaho Falls, Idaho

Heart Stroganoff

6 fresh mushrooms,
  sliced
1 medium onion,
  chopped
2 tbsp. margarine or
  butter
2 tbsp. vegetable oil
2 lbs. venison or elk
  heart, cut into strips
  ¹/₂-inch thick
Flour
2 cups beef broth
1 cup commercial sour
  cream
Salt and pepper to taste

Sauté mushrooms and onion in butter. Remove and set aside. Add 2 tbsp. oil to pan. Shake the meat in flour and brown in oil. Add broth and simmer about 1¹/₄ hours. Then add the mushrooms, onion, and sour cream. Stir together and heat until hot. Season with salt and pepper. This is good served over noodles or rice. Serves 8-10.

Karen Kmet
Clancy, Montana

SQUASH CASSEROLE WITH WILD GAME SAUSAGE

3 yellow squash, sliced
I lb. wild game sausage
   or pork sausage,
   crumbled or sliced
I cup chopped red onion
I egg
¼ cup milk
I cup bread crumbs
¼ cup parmesan cheese

Parboil squash until crisp-tender; drain. Cook sausage until done; drain. Cook onions in some of the sausage grease until translucent. Place squash in 8-9-inch oven dish. Add sausages and onion. Mix egg and milk. Pour over casserole. Mix bread crumbs and cheese, sprinkle over top. Bake at 350 degrees about 25 minutes. Serves 3-4.

Debby Talley
Hobbs, New Mexico

WILD SAUSAGE CASSEROLE

I lb. dried lima beans
6 cups water
I tsp. salt
I tsp. pepper
I clove garlic, minced
2 slices bacon, cut-up
¼ cup chopped celery
¼ cup chopped green
   pepper
¼ cup chopped onion
¼ cup chili sauce
2 cans tomato paste
   (6 oz. each)
⅛ tsp dried basil
⅛ tsp. mace
I tbsp. Worcestershire
   sauce
6 wild game sausage
   links, sliced

Soak lima beans overnight in water to cover. Drain, then add 6 cups water, salt, pepper, and minced garlic. Cook until tender, 1½-2 hours. Drain. Mix with remaining ingredients. Put in casserole and bake at 350 degrees for 1 hour or cook in slow cooker 4-6 hours. Serves 6.

Harriet Parks
Alpine, Wyoming

KNUCKYS AND ELK MEAT SAUCE

SAUCE:
2 lbs. elk burger
2 cups mushrooms,
    chopped
1 green pepper, chopped
1 onion, chopped and
    sautéed
3-4 garlic cloves,
    chopped
2 cans tomatoes
    (28 oz. each)
2 cans tomato paste
    (6 oz. each)
1 can tomato sauce
    (8 oz.)
1 tbsp. dried oregano
1 tbsp. dried basil
Salt and pepper to tase
Pinch of nutmeg

KNUCKY DUMPLINGS:
6 potatoes
Flour

Brown burger in small amount of oil. Remove. Add mushrooms, peppers, onion, and garlic and cook until onions are translucent. Add remaining sauce ingredients and simmer 2 hours. Peel and boil 6 potatoes just until able to pierce with fork. Drain. Mash and let cool. Mix cold potatoes with enough flour to make a dough the consistency of bread dough. Roll out and cut in cubes. Put in boiling water. Cook until they float to the top. Remove. Put in pan with sauce and sprinkle with grated cheddar cheese. Serves 6-8.

Yvonne Cenorerine
Winfield, British Columbia

Venison Marinade

1 1/2 cups oil
3/4 cup soy sauce
2 tbsp. Worcestershire
    sauce
2 tbsp. dry mustard
2 tbsp. salt
1 tbsp. pepper
1 cup dry red wine
1 tsp. dried parsley
    flakes
1/3 cup lemon juice

Put ingredients into a 1-quart jar and shake well. Makes 3 1/2 cups.

Lorna Dorey
Rocky Mountain House
Alberta

California Meat Marinade

1 cup soy sauce
1 cup sherry
1/4 cup lemon juice
2 cloves garlic, crushed
1-inch piece fresh ginger,
    peeled and grated
    (or use 1 tsp. ground
    ginger)

Mix all ingredients. Use to marinate roasts, steaks, or any game. Marinate at least 4 hours in refrigerator; overnight is better. Baste meat with marinade while cooking. Makes 2 1/4 cups.

Lynnel Pollock
Woodland, California

JERKY

1 1/2 lbs. ground elk,
venison, bear,
or moose
1 tsp. Liquid Smoke
1 tsp. salt
1 tsp. onion powder
1/3 tsp. garlic powder
1/4 cup soy sauce
1/4 cup Worcestershire
sauce
1 tsp. Cajun seasoning

Mix all ingredients in bowl. Place between two sheets of wax paper. Using a rolling pin, roll to 1/8-inch thickness. Cut in strips 2 x 4-inches. Place on foil-lined cookie sheet. Dry in oven at 150 degrees 8-12 hours.

NOTE: A hint from Ann Canape of Evergreen, Colorado, is to hang strips across oven rack using paper clips.

Roger T. Troxell
Glasgow, Pennsylvania

STEVE'S ELK JERKY

Seasoning salt and black
pepper to taste
3-4 lbs. elk or moose
meat, sliced into thin
strips

MARINADE:
1 tbsp. salt
1 1/2 tsp. onion powder
1 tsp. MSG
1 1/2 tsp. garlic powder
1/2 tsp. pepper
2 tbsp. Liquid Smoke
1 tbsp. sugar
1 cup warm water
1 tsp. red pepper

Dissolve marinade seasonings in warm water. Place marinade and meat strips in a deep glass pan, cover, and marinate for 12-24 hours in refrigerator. Turn meat in dish every 4 hours. Remove meat. Pat meat dry with paper towels to remove extra moisture. Add seasoning salt and fresh ground pepper to taste. Line bottom of oven with foil and hang meat strips directly from oven racks (or lay on cookie sheet). Set oven at 150 degrees. Cook meat for about 4 hours, checking often for dryness. Steve says the more red pepper you add to the recipe, the more beer you have to drink when you eat the jerky!

Vardis Fisher

OVEN-BAKED SALAMI

**5 lbs. lean ground
venison**
**5 tsp. Morton Tender
Quick salt**
**1 tsp. Liquid Smoke or
hickory smoked salt**
2¹/₂ tsp. mustard seed
2¹/₂ tsp. garlic salt
**2¹/₂ tsp. black
peppercorns**

Mix all ingredients well, cover, and refrigerate for 2-3 days. Divide meat into 8 equal-sized meatballs. Take each meatball and roll out on floured table top to make it look like a big cigar. Place all 8 salamis on a broiler pan and bake at 150 degrees for 4-8 hours. Turn every ¹/₂ hour. After 4 hours they are usually done. Cut one to test. Outside will start to dry and become firm, but inside should be moist. Best when still warm from the oven. After cooling, can be wrapped and frozen. Makes 8.

*John Zanon
Norway, Michigan*

Elk Salami

2¹/₂ lbs. coarse ground elk

¹/₄ tsp. coarse ground pepper

¹/₄ tsp. fine ground pepper

¹/₂ tsp. minced garlic flakes

¹/₂ tsp. minced onion flakes

2 heaping tbsp. Morton Tender Quick salt

Combine all ingredients well by hand. Shape into 3 rolls, wrap in foil, twist ends tight. Refrigerate 24 hours. Leave wrapped in foil and boil in large kettle for 17 minutes. Remove, unwrap, let cool. If not serving right away, rewrap in plastic wrap and store in freezer.

NOTE: Sue Gooding bakes her salami in 150-200 degree oven for 8 hours. She perforates the foil rolls several times and places them on a broiler pan so fat can drip down to bottom.

Chuck and Margie Fraser
Lakeside, Montana

Italian Sausage

2 lbs. pork shoulder

4 lbs. elk, venison, or antelope

1¹/₂ tbsp. coarse black pepper

1¹/₂ tbsp. salt

2 tbsp. anise seed

3 tbsp. Italian seasoning

Dashes of onion powder and garlic powder

Coarse grind pork and game meat. Add all other ingredients and blend well. Refrigerate overnight to enhance flavor. Mixture may be stuffed in casings or left in bulk for patties. Makes 6 pounds.

Tom Canape
Evergreen, Colorado

Pepperoni

4-5 lbs. elk or venison burger
1 envelope Good Seasons Italian Dressing Mix (dissolved in ¹/₂ cup water)
1 tbsp. smoked salt
1 tbsp. coarse ground pepper
1 tbsp. red pepper flakes (optional)
3 tbsp. Morton's Tender Quick curing salt
1 tsp. anise seed
¹/₂ tsp. anise extract
1 tsp. cumin powder
1 tsp. onion powder
1 tsp. garlic powder
1 tbsp. Worcestershire sauce

In a large mixing bowl, combine all of the ingredients and mix well to blend. Cover and refrigerate overnight. Remove from the refrigerator and knead like bread dough once a day for the next three days. On the last day, divide and form into rolls. Place each roll on a broiler rack or pan. Place in a preheated 150-degree oven and bake 8-8¹/₂ hours, turning several times for even baking. Can be refrigerated or frozen for later use.

Ferrol Dene Baldwin
Cedar City, Utah

BOAR SAUSAGE STUFFING

1 lb. boar sausage
1 medium onion,
   chopped
1/2 cup butter or
   margarine
2 tbsp. chopped fresh
   parsley
1 tsp. ground sage
1 tsp. crushed thyme
1 tsp. dried rosemary
1 tbsp. Mrs. Dash
1/2 cup sliced almonds
1/2 cup raisins
1 medium apple,
   chopped
12 cups dried bread
   cubes
1 cup hot water
1 chicken bouillon cube

Brown boar sausage and onion in butter. Add remaining ingredients except water and bouillon cube. Mix water and bouillon cube and add to mixture. Makes enough stuffing for a 10-12 pound wild turkey.

Margaret C. Robinson
Pelham, New Hampshire

CANNED VENISON

Preparation of the venison before canning is a vital step. Aging is not necessary at all, but you must carefully cube the meat (from any part of the deer), removing all the fat and sinew. Once the meat has been cubed, the rest is easy. First, you stuff the meat tightly into mason jars, leaving an inch or so at the top. Then add 1 tbsp. of water, salt (optional), and 1 beef bouillon cube. Also, you can add your own favorite spices if you want to experiment. Next, loosely tighten the lids and pressure cook the venison in water for approximately 1-2 hours. When the 2 hours are up, you remove the jars and let them cool until the lids seal. (If a jar doesn't seal, put it in the refrigerator and you'll have your meat for tonight.)

David Lackey
River Falls, Wisconsin

EDITOR'S NOTE: Please check canning instructions with your pressure cooker to be sure you are doing everything correctly.

TERIYAKI STEAK SAUCE

1 tbsp. fresh ginger,
　chopped fine, or
　2 tsp. powdered
　ginger
1 tbsp. fresh garlic,
　chopped fine
2 tbsp. sugar
1/4 cup water
1/2 cup soy sauce

Combine ingredients, pour over steak, and let stand several hours before cooking by your favorite method.

Lorna Dorey
Rocky Mountain House
Alberta

CORNISH MEAT PASTIES

1/2 lb. elk or venison,
　cut into 1/4-inch cubes
1/2 cup raw potato,
　cut into 1/4-inch cubes
1/4 cup onion, chopped
1 tsp. salt
1/8 tsp. pepper
1 tsp. dried parsley
　flakes
Dash dried thyme
1 tbsp. water
1 tsp. Worcestershire
　sauce
1 recipe pastry
　(2-crust pie)

Mix together meat, potato cubes, onion, salt, pepper, parsley, and thyme. Add water and Worcestershire sauce. Toss until moistened. Prepare pastry. Divide into 8 equal portions. Roll out each on a floured board to a 5-inch circle. Place 1/8 of meat mixture on each pastry circle. Moisten edges of pastry circles with water. Fold pastry over meat mixture and seal edges. Place on ungreased cookie sheet. Bake at 400 degrees for 25-30 minutes or until pastry is golden brown. Serve hot or cold. Makes 8.

Barbara J. Nelson
Salinas, California

SMOTHERED GREEN CHILE BURRITOS

2 lbs. elk meat (any cut just as long as it's elk and well trimmed), cut into small chunks
1 cup flour
6-7 tbsp. vegetable oil
2 medium onions, diced
1 can diced green chilies (7 oz.)
2 cans diced jalapeño peppers (3 oz. each)
2 cups milk
1 tsp. salt (optional)
1 tsp. cumin
1/2 tsp. pepper
1/2 tsp. garlic salt
1/4 tsp. oregano
1 lb. cheddar cheese, grated
1 lb. Monterey jack cheese, grated
24 flour tortillas, 6-inch size

Coat meat in 1/2 cup flour and brown in large skillet with 1/4 cup vegetable oil over medium high heat. Reduce heat and add onions, half of the green chilies, and 2 oz. jalapeños, or 3 oz. for a spicier flavor. Simmer for 10-15 minutes. Drain excess fat. In a separate large skillet, add 2-3 tbsp. vegetable oil and heat over medium high heat. Add 1/2 cup flour and stir a few minutes until flour gets cooked. Add milk slowly, stirring constantly with a whisk. As mixture thickens, add remaining green chilies, salt, cumin, pepper, garlic salt, and oregano. Heat thoroughly. Add a third of the meat mixture and cook to the consistency of gravy. Meanwhile, have the tortillas at room temperature to prevent cracking. Spoon 2 tbsp. of meat mixture and 1 tbsp. each of cheddar cheese and Monterey jack cheese onto a tortilla. Roll up and place seam side down in a large rectangular cake pan (you may need 2 pans). Prepare remaining tortillas in the same manner in a single layer. Cover all burritos with the gravy mixture and top with the rest of the cheeses. Cover and bake at 350 degrees for 15-20 minutes. Serve with Spanish rice and guacamole. Serves 6-8.

Welden Schneider
Fort Morgan, Colorado

Wild Game Vegetable Kabobs

MARINADE:
1 cup red wine
¼ cup oil
1 clove garlic, minced
½ large onion, minced
½ tsp. freshly ground
   pepper
2 tbsp. soy sauce
¼-½ tsp. dry mustard
½ tsp. Italian seasoning

KABOBS:
2 lbs. wild game meat,
   cut in squares
Vegetable chunks or
   slices, as desired:
   fresh mushrooms,
   cherry tomatoes,
   onion, zucchini, red
   and green peppers

Marinate meat in refrigerator for 1-6 hours, depending on toughness of cut. Alternate vegetables and meat on metal skewers. Barbecue 15-20 minutes, or until done. Turn and baste frequently with marinade. The marinade is also good for roasts. Serves 6.

Linda Ward
Missoula, Montana

TERIYAKI ELK KABOBS

1½ lbs. elk steak, cubed

2 green peppers, cubed

15 cherry tomatoes

Zucchini, cucumber, olives, red peppers, or canned artichokes; cut into uniform size before using

½ lb. fresh mushrooms, whole if small, cut in half if large

TERIYAKI MARINADE:

½ cup soy sauce

2 tbsp. molasses

¼ cup salad oil

2 tsp. ground ginger

2 tsp. dry mustard

6 garlic cloves, minced

Marinate meat for 15 minutes. Drain. Place ingredients on metal skewers, alternating meat with fresh vegetables. Grill 5 to 10 minutes, turning frequently and basting with marinade. Serves 6.

EDITOR'S NOTE: I find it works better to put each type of vegetable on its own skewer and meat on its own skewer. This way meat gets done, and vegetables don't overcook.

Debora Ann Petty
Columbia Falls, Montana

Sweet and Sour Rabbit

2-3 lbs. rabbit, disjointed
Tempura batter mix
(prepare according to
directions)
Peanut oil for deep
frying
1 cup pineapple juice
¼ cup vinegar
1 cup pineapple chunks
1 green pepper, sliced
½ tbsp. cornstarch
½ cup sugar
½ cup water
Salt and pepper

Heat oil, dip rabbit pieces in batter, deep fry. Remove pieces and drain. Mix pineapple juice and vinegar, cook a few minutes. Add pineapple and green pepper, cook a few minutes more. Mix cornstarch and sugar in water and add to pan. Add rabbit pieces, cook until sauce thickens. Salt and pepper to taste. Serves 4-6.

Richard Beardsley
Boulder, Colorado

Sweet and Sour Elk

2 lbs. boneless elk meat,
  cut into ¹/₂-inch cubes
¹/₄ cup soy sauce
Cornstarch
Flour
3 beaten eggs
Oil for frying
1 large onion, cubed
1 large green pepper,
  cubed
6 large mushrooms,
  quartered
1 can pineapple chunks,
  drained (5¹/₂ oz.);
  reserve the juice

Sauce:
¹/₂ cup pineapple juice
¹/₄ cup wine vinegar
2 tbsp. oil
2 tbsp. brown sugar
1 tbsp. soy sauce
¹/₂ tsp. black pepper
1 tsp. cornstarch
2 tsp. water

Marinate meat cubes in soy sauce for a few minutes. Sprinkle cornstarch and flour on separate plates. Lightly roll meat in cornstarch, dip in egg, and then in flour. Fry in hot oil until brown. Drain on paper towels and keep warm. Heat small amount of oil in cast-iron skillet or wok and add onions and green pepper. Stir and fry until just tender. Add mushrooms and cook a few minutes more, then add pineapple chunks and browned meat cubes and heat thoroughly.

Sauce: Combine pineapple juice, vinegar, oil, brown sugar, soy sauce, and pepper in small saucepan. Heat to a boil. Mix cornstarch and water and add to pan. Cook to desired thickness. Pour sweet and sour sauce over meat and vegetables and stir well. Serve on steamed rice. Serves 8-12.

Ken Kneeland
Golden, Colorado

VENISON STIR-FRY

$\frac{1}{3}$ cup beef or chicken broth

2 tbsp. soy sauce

3 tbsp. orange marmalade

1 tbsp. cornstarch

1 lb. boneless venison, trimmed of fat

2 tbsp. minced fresh ginger

3 tbsp. oil

1 medium onion, cut into 1-inch wedges

$\frac{3}{4}$ lb. snow peas, ends and strings removed

Combine $\frac{1}{4}$ cup broth, soy sauce, and marmalade. In another cup, mix remaining broth with cornstarch until blended. Rinse venison and pat dry. Cut meat across the grain into $\frac{1}{8}$-inch thick slanting slices, each about 2 inches long. Mix pieces with ginger. Place wok or 10-12-inch frying pan over high heat. When hot, add 1 tbsp. oil. When oil is hot, add onion. Stir-fry until onion is just lightly tinged with brown but still crisp, about 2 minutes; pour onion from pan and set aside. Add another 1 tbsp. oil to the pan. When hot, add half of the venison mixture and stir-fry until meat is lightly browned, about 2 minutes. Add to onions. Repeat, using remaining 1 tbsp. oil and venison mixture; add to meat and onions. Pour marmalade mixture into wok, add snow peas and stir until they turn bright green, about 2 minutes. Add meat, onions, and cornstarch mixture to pan; stir until boiling. Serve with steamed rice. Serves 4.

Shelley Gilligan
Hillsborough, California

Spicy Stir-fried Venison

1 lb. lean venison,
  cut into 1-inch pieces
2 green peppers
2 medium onions
¹/₂ lb. fresh mushrooms
Cajun blackened
  seasoning
Worcestershire sauce
Vegetable (not olive) oil
2 cups cooked rice

Slice peppers, onions, and mushrooms into bite-sized pieces for individual servings. Preheat deep-dish fry pan with 1 tbsp. oil, and heat until a drop of water sizzles in oil. Add ¹/₄ lb. venison and stir until the meat browns. Add 1 tbsp. Worcestershire sauce and ¹/₄ of the peppers, onions, and mushrooms. Stir occasionally and add Cajun seasoning to flavor, usually ¹/₂-1 tsp. is sufficient. Cook just long enough for peppers to remain crunchy. Remove from heat and serve over a bed of cooked rice. Rice can be flavored with bouillon cube, diced mushrooms, or chives to add extra flavor. Salt and pepper to taste. Serves 4.

NOTE: Each serving must be made separately because most deep fry pans cannot accommodate more than one serving at a time. If you have a large wok, 4 servings could be made at once.

Tom Canape
Evergreen, Colorado

FISH

NOTT'S STEELHEAD DELIGHT

**1 20-lb. Steelhead
(or two 10-pounders)**
8-10 slices bacon
4-5 lemons

OYSTER STUFFING:
**15-20 medium-sized
fresh mushrooms,
sliced**
**1 tbsp. butter or
margarine**
⅛ tsp. garlic powder
Salt and pepper
**1 loaf white bread, cut
into cubes**
**2 jars medium oysters
(10 oz.)**
4 stalks celery, chopped
1 onion, diced
**1 tbsp. dried parsley
flakes**

Sauté mushrooms in butter or margarine, add garlic and dash of salt and pepper. Add mushrooms to bread in large mixing bowl. Drain and rinse oysters, chop, then add to mixture. Add celery, onion, and parsley flakes to mixture. Mix by hand. Cover mixture and put in refrigerator overnight.

THE NEXT DAY: Rinse steelhead with baking soda inside and out (we find that this kills the fishy taste). Drain excess water from fish. Stuff fish with your stuffing mixture, making sure to pack the steelhead firmly and full. Drape bacon over steelhead. Slice lemons and put slices in between bacon strips. Wrap steelhead in heavy aluminum foil and bake at 350 degrees until steelhead is flaky at a fork's probe (about 1½ hours). Serves about 30.

*Douglas Nott
Yakima, Washington*

Finger Suckin' Salmon

Salmon, cut into chunks
Salt brine
Garlic powder
Black pepper
Brown sugar
Ketchup
Prepared mustard
Worcestershire sauce
Tabasco

Soak fish chunks in salt brine overnight, then drain. Place pieces on smoking racks in an oven, over a pan that will catch the drippings. Bake at 350 degrees for 20-30 minutes, or until they appear to be nearly cooked, but not quite. Meanwhile, mix all ingredients in a bowl, to your satisfaction. The mix should have a thick consistency and be able to coat the fish without running off. Pat dry the now-baked fish and coat both sides with the mixture, then place the racks in a smoker. The fish needs to smoke for only about 6-7 hours to finish cooking and also to bake the mixture into the flesh. When prepared in this way, the fish doesn't have that dried-out texture, and is quite moist. You cut down considerably on your smoking time, and you will never smoke fish any other way again.

Rick Anzalone
Chehalis, Washington

BAKED WHOLE SALMON

1 salmon (7-10 lbs.)
³/₄ cup dry white wine
¹/₄ tsp. dried rosemary
¹/₄ tsp. dried tarragon
3 green onions, minced
3 peppercorns
¹/₄ tsp. dried thyme
¹/₂ tsp. dried basil
Celery leaves
2 slices lemon

Put wine and all remaining ingredients, except salmon, in a covered saucepan and heat without boiling for 30 minutes. Rinse salmon, pat dry. Remove the tail and lay fish lengthwise on a sheet of foil. Pour warm herb-wine over and inside the fish. Bring foil up over the fish and seal by crimping. Be sure no liquid can escape. Place on a baking sheet and bake at 350 degrees 12-15 minutes per pound or about 1¹/₂ hours. Do not overbake. Can be served hot or cold. Serves 12-15.

Bernis Wagner
Roseburg, Oregon

SALMON LOAF

12 oz. cooked salmon
$^1/_2$ cup evaporated milk
$^1/_2$ cup bread crumbs
2 eggs, slightly beaten
$^1/_2$ cup green onion,
    chopped
$^1/_4$ tsp. dried thyme
Salt and pepper
1 tbsp. margarine

Mix all but margarine. Pat into loaf pan and dot mixture with margarine. Bake at 350 degrees for 45 minutes or microwave on medium high for 18 minutes. Serves 6.

Yvonne Decker
Libby, Montana

CURRY OF FRESH SALMON

4 salmon steaks,
8 oz. each
1 cup salted water
4 tbsp. butter
¼ lb. mushrooms, sliced
2 tbsp. minced green
pepper
½ tsp. ground coriander
1 tsp. turmeric
2 tsp. ground cumin
1¼ tsp. ground ginger
½ tsp. finely minced chili
pepper
3 tbsp. flour
2 cups hot milk
8 green onions, sliced
Salt to taste

Poach salmon in 1 cup salted water for 7-10 minutes, until tender. Drain, remove all skin and bones, and cut salmon into 1-inch cubes. Set aside. Melt butter in heavy saucepan over low flame, add mushrooms, green pepper, coriander, turmeric, cumin, ginger, and chili pepper, mix well, and sauté until mushrooms are tender. Stir in flour, mixing very well, and then slowly stir in hot milk. Cook sauce until thickened. Add salmon, green onions, and salt to taste, simmer 5 minutes, and serve with rice. Serves 4-6.

Judy Reed
Missoula, Montana

SALMON CAKES

2 eggs
2 tbsp. milk
1 can red salmon,
   drained (15¹/₂ oz.)
1 tbsp. mayonnaise or
   salad dressing
1 tbsp. prepared
   mustard
1 cup bread crumbs
2 tbsp. seafood
   seasoning
Oil for frying

In large mixing bowl, beat eggs and milk together. Add mustard, mayonnaise or salad dressing, and salmon. Then add bread crumbs and seasoning. Form into patties and fry in skillet with oil. Serves 4-6.

Carol Sue Kehs
Stevensville, Montana

SALMON PIE

1 can red salmon
(15½ oz.)
3 eggs, beaten
1 cup sour cream
½ cup grated sharp
cheddar cheese
¼ cup mayonnaise
1 tbsp. grated onion
3 drops hot sauce
¼ tsp. dried dill weed
½ lb. mushrooms,
sautéed
3-4 green onions,
chopped

CRUST:
1½ cups whole-wheat
flour
1 cup grated cheddar
cheese
½ tsp. salt
½ tsp. paprika
½ cup butter, softened
⅓ cup chopped almonds

Mix flour, cheese, salt, and paprika in bowl. Cut in butter until crumbly. Add almonds. Set 1 cup of crust aside for topping. Press remaining crust into a 9-inch pie plate.

Drain and flake salmon, removing bones. Save liquid. Add liquid, beaten eggs, sour cream, cheese, mayonnaise, and grated onion, hot sauce, and dill to salmon, mixing thoroughly. Fold in mushrooms and green onions. Turn into crust. Sprinkle with reserved crumbs. Bake about 45 minutes at 400 degrees. Serves 6.

Ruth Saholt
Whitefish, Montana

SEA SCALLOPS WITH WINE

1 lb. sea scallops
¹/₂ tsp. salt
¹/₃ tsp. black pepper
Flour
4 tbsp. butter
¹/₄ cup dry white wine
Juice of one lemon
¹/₈ tsp. dried basil

Salt and pepper, then dust scallops lightly with flour. Sauté in butter until light brown on both sides. Add wine, lemon juice, and basil. Cook about 7 minutes more. Do not overcook. Serves 4.

Jann Weber

RICE STUFFING FOR WHOLE FISH

¹/₂ cup melted butter
1 cup chopped onion
2 cups diced celery
1 cup canned drained
　mushrooms, sliced
3 cups cooked rice
¹/₂ cup green pepper,
　chopped
Salt
Pepper
¹/₂ tsp. dried marjoram
¹/₄ tsp. dried thyme

Melt butter and sauté onion, celery, mushrooms, and green pepper until tender. Add sautéed vegetable mixture to cooked rice along with seasonings. Sprinkle inside of fish with salt. Stuff fish loosely with rice mixture and secure with skewers. If using aluminum foil, oil foil on one side. Wrap fish in foil, oiled side next to fish. Bake at 450 degrees for 15 minutes, plus 10 minutes for each inch of fish thickness. Makes 7 cups of stuffing.

Lorna Dorey
Rocky Mountain House,
Alberta

KWIK KIWI TROUT OR SALMON

**2 trout fillets, 2-3 lb., or
1 salmon fillet, 3-5 lb.**
**2 green onions, finely
sliced**
Juice of 1/2 orange
Juice of 1/2 lemon
Lemon slices
1/2 tsp. soy sauce
2 kiwis
Pepper to taste
Paprika to taste
Garlic powder to taste

Arrange fillets in shallow, foil-lined baking dish. Peel and mash kiwis and mix with onion, soy sauce, and orange and lemon juice. Pour over fish and sprinkle with seasonings. Bake 30 minutes at 400 degrees. Remove fish to serving platter. Garnish with fresh parsley and lemon slices. Serves 8-10.

Lynne Egan
Clancy, Montana

TROUT-A-RUDIES (TROUT OMELET)

1 large trout, cooked
1/2 large onion, diced
1/4 lb. bacon, diced
1 clove garlic, minced
1 large tomato, diced
6 eggs
1/4 cup half-and-half
1 tsp. hot sauce
Salt and pepper to taste
**2 cups grated
hot pepper cheese**

Flake fish from bones and set aside. Sauté onion and bacon in skillet until onion is soft; add garlic and tomato and sauté briefly. Set aside. Whisk together eggs, half-and-half, hot sauce, salt, and pepper. Add to large, lightly oiled skillet. Cook over low heat until eggs are slightly set. Add onion mixture and fish flakes to one side of egg. Cover and cook about 5 minutes over very low heat. Fold egg mixture in half to cover fish and onion. Cover with cheese, cover skillet, and cook until cheese melts. Serves 6.

Gracene Long
Hamilton, Montana

LOW-CALORIE TROUT SANDWICH SPREAD

1 cup flaked cooked
   trout
¹/₃ cup low-calorie ranch
   dressing
2 green onions, minced
1 tsp. pickle relish
1 small tomato, diced
¹/₂ small stalk celery,
   diced

Combine ingredients and mix well. Spread between two slices of bread along with low-calorie cream cheese and sliced cucumber. Makes about 1¹/₂ cups.

Gracene Long
Hamilton, Montana

Fresh Trout a la Creole

1/4 cup butter
4-5 green onions,
     chopped, including
     green part
2 cloves garlic, minced
1/2 green pepper,
     chopped
1 stalk celery, finely
     chopped
2 tbsp. flour
1 can tomatoes (16 oz.),
     chopped, with liquid
1 can tomato paste
     (6 oz.)
2 tbsp. fresh parsley,
     chopped
2 bay leaves
1 tsp. dried thyme
1/4-1/2 tsp. cayenne
     pepper
1 tsp. dried tarragon
Juice of 1/2 lemon
1/2 cup dry white wine
Salt and pepper to taste
4 medium trout

Melt butter in saucepan and add onion, garlic, green pepper, and celery; sauté until onions are transparent and tender. Add the flour to make a paste. Add the chopped tomatoes, including liquid, and tomato paste. Add enough water to make a sauce. Add parsley, bay leaves, thyme, cayenne, tarragon, lemon juice, and wine. Simmer for at least 30 minutes. Add salt and pepper to taste. Place trout in a buttered casserole. Pour Creole sauce over fish to cover. Bake 30-45 minutes at 350 degrees. Serve with rice. Salmon may be used in place of trout. Serves 4.

Mary Ann Bigelow
Missoula, Montana

CREAMED POACHED MONTANA TROUT

4 cups heavy cream
1 cup finely diced carrot
1/2 cup finely diced celery
1/2 cup finely diced green
   onion
1 tbsp. minced parsley
6 trout, cleaned,
   6-8 oz. each

In a large skillet, bring cream to a simmer. Add vegetables and cook 5 minutes. Lay trout in sauce and poach 5-7 minutes or until fish flakes easily from the bone. Keep each trout warm in oven until all are cooked. Serves 6.

Frank L. Sonnenberg
Missoula, Montana

PICKLED MONTANA TROUT

20 medium trout
2 large onions, sliced
3 cups white vinegar
1 cup water
3/4 cup sugar
1 1/2 tbsp. plain or
   pickling salt
   (non-iodized)
2 cloves garlic
2 tbsp. pickling spices

Clean, skin, and cut up trout into 2-inch pieces. Put in large pan and cover with water. Bring to a boil and cook 3 minutes. Drain. Pack fish with sliced onion into sterilized quart jars. Combine vinegar, water, sugar, salt, garlic, and spices in saucepan and boil together 15 minutes. Pour hot syrup over fish in jars and seal. Let stand in jars 2-3 days or longer before using. Makes about 10 quarts.

Ann Harding
Philipsburg, Montana

Montana Canned Trout

6 trout (2-6 lbs.)
7 tsp. vinegar
7 tsp. canning salt

While fish are partially frozen, scale and cut off fins, heads, and tails. Slice into 1-1¹/₂-inch pieces. Pack into hot, sterilized pint jars. Add 1 tsp. salt and 1 tsp. vinegar to each jar. Seal jars and put in boiling water just to cover jars. Boil 4 hours. Age 30 days before using. Fish also can be cooked for 1 hour 40 minutes in a pressure cooker at 10 lbs. pressure. Makes 7 pints.

VARIATION: Judy Kuhl of Helena, Montana, places in each jar along with fish, 1 tsp. canning salt, 3 tbsp. spicy tomato juice, 4 tbsp. vinegar, ¹/₄ tsp. Worcestershire sauce, and 1 tsp. cooking oil. Cook as above.

Gertrude Thornton
Helena, Montana

PICKLED PADDLEFISH

Paddlefish, cleaned and
cut into 1 1/2-2-inch
chunks
Salt water
White vinegar
2-3 large onions, sliced
1/2 large lemon, sliced

BRINE:

3 cups white vinegar
3 cups sugar
1 1/2 cups white wine
4 dried red chili peppers
1/3 cup pickling spice
1/4 tsp. mustard seed
1/4 tsp. celery seed

Pack fish chunks into a gallon jar, filling almost to top. Pour in salt water strong enough to float an egg. Soak 24 hours in refrigerator. Drain but do not rinse. Soak another 24 hours in refrigerator in white vinegar. Drain again but do not rinse. Put all brine ingredients into a kettle, stirring to dissolve the sugar. Bring to a boil, remove from heat, and let cool. Remove fish from jar. Layer fish, onion slices, and lemon slices in jar until jar is full. Press fish down gently and cover with brine. Refrigerate 20 days. Trout may be used in place of paddlefish. Makes 1 gallon.

Marlyse Drogitis
Harrison, Montana

Stuffed Baked Bass

1 bass, cleaned (3-4 lb.)
Salt and pepper to taste
4 cups coarse dry bread
  crumbs
1/2 cup finely chopped
  onion
1 tsp. salt (optional)
1/8 tsp. pepper
2 eggs, beaten
1/2 cup butter, melted
1/2 tsp. ground cloves
4 tbsp. port wine
4 tbsp. ketchup
2 tbsp. water
2 tbsp. lemon juice
1 cup fine bread crumbs
2 tbsp. butter, melted
Lemon slices
Parsley

Wash fish and dry well. Remove head and tail if desired. Sprinkle cavity with salt and pepper and lay fish in buttered baking dish. In a large bowl, combine next 7 ingredients, tossing lightly. Stuff the fish cavity with this mixture; use small skewers to hold cavity closed. Combine wine, ketchup, water, and lemon juice. Pour half of this over the fish. Bake at 375 degrees, 12 minutes per pound or until fish flakes easily with a fork. Remove fish from oven. Combine fine bread crumbs and 2 tbsp. melted butter and sprinkle over fish. Return fish to 400-degree oven and bake until crumbs are lightly browned, about 5 minutes. Garnish with lemon slices and parsley. Serves 6-8.

Elaine Kyriss
Billings, Montana

DESSERTS

No-bake Cocoa Chewies

¹/₄ cup margarine
2 cups sugar
¹/₄ cup cocoa
¹/₂ cup milk
1 tsp. vanilla
3 cups rolled oats,
   uncooked

Simmer margarine, sugar, cocoa, and milk for 1 minute. Add vanilla and oatmeal. Stir together and drop by spoonfuls onto wax paper. Allow to cool.

Sharon Robertson
Kansas City, Kansas

7-Layer Bars

8 tbsp. butter (1 stick)
1 cup graham cracker
   crumbs
1 cup coconut, shredded
1 pkg. chocolate chips
   (12 oz.)
1 pkg. butterscotch
   chips (12 oz.)
1 can sweetened
   condensed milk
   (14 oz.)
1 tsp. vanilla
1 cup chopped nuts

Melt butter, pour in 9 x 13-inch pan. Layer ingredients in the following order: cracker crumbs, coconut, chocolate chips, butterscotch chips, milk and vanilla mixed, and nuts.

Bake at 325 degrees for 30 minutes. Serves 12-20.

Ann Porter
Pleasant Hill, Missouri

OATMEAL SCOTCHIE BARS

1 cup flour
1 tsp. baking soda
1/2 tsp. salt
1/2 tsp. cinnamon
1 cup butter, softened
3/4 cup sugar
3/4 cup firmly packed
   brown sugar
2 eggs
1 tsp. vanilla extract
3 cups rolled oats,
   uncooked
2 cups butterscotch
   morsels

Preheat oven to 375 degrees. In small bowl, combine flour, baking soda, salt, and cinnamon. Set aside. In large mixer bowl, cream butter, sugar, brown sugar, eggs, vanilla. Beat well. Gradually add flour mixture. Stir in oats and butterscotch morsels. Spread the dough into a greased 15 x 10 x 1-inch baking pan. Bake at 375 degrees for 20-25 minutes. Cool completely. Cut into 35 2-inch squares.

Sharon Robertson
Kansas City, Kansas

LIFESAVER BARS

3-4 cups graham cracker
   crumbs
1/2 cup butter or
   margarine, softened
1 cup walnuts, chopped
1 cup coconut
1 cup semi-sweet
   chocolate chips
1 can sweetened
   condensed milk
   (14 oz.)

Work graham cracker crumbs and butter together. Press into bottom of a 9 x 13-inch baking pan. Mix walnuts, coconut, and chocolate chips together. Scatter over crust. Drizzle condensed milk over top. Bake at 350 degrees for 1/2 hour. Best kept frozen. Serves 12-20.

Anna Wolterson
Cranbrook, British Columbia

MALTED-MILK BROWNIES

1³/₄ cup flour
³/₄ cup cocoa
¹/₂ cup malted milk
   powder
1 tsp. baking powder
³/₄ tsp. salt
6 oz. unsalted butter,
   melted
1³/₄ cups sugar
1 tsp. vanilla
3 eggs
1 cup chocolate covered
   malted milk balls,
   chopped

Mix flour, cocoa, malted milk powder, baking powder, and salt. Stir sugar and vanilla into melted butter. Beat in eggs one at a time. Add flour mixture and chopped malted milk balls and mix. Pour into greased 13 x 9-inch pan. Bake at 325 degrees for 30 to 35 minutes. Serves 18 or more.

Yvonne Decker
Libby, Montana

BROWNIES FOR A CROWD

1¹/₂ cups flour
1 tsp. salt
2 cups sugar
8 tbsp. cocoa (¹/₂ cup)
1 tsp. vanilla
1 cup vegetable oil
4 eggs
¹/₄ cup water
2 cups chopped walnuts

FROSTING:
¹/₄ cup water
12 large marshmallows
3 tbsp. cocoa
1¹/₂ cup powdered sugar
1 tsp. vanilla

Mix first eight ingredients together. Stir in nuts. Pour into 11 x 15-inch greased pan. Bake at 350 degrees for 30 minutes.

Heat water, marshmallows, and cocoa in a double boiler (or microwave) until marshmallows are melted. Cool. Add sugar and vanilla. Beat until of spreading consistency. Spread over brownies. Makes 45 brownies.

Patty Bogh
McMinnville, Oregon

Dona's applesauce Cake

2¹/₂ cups applesauce
4 tsp. baking soda
2 cups raisins
2 cups brown sugar
1 cup shortening
2 eggs
3 cups flour
1 tsp. cinnamon
1 tsp. nutmeg
¹/₂ tsp. salt
1 cup nuts, chopped

Stir raisins, applesauce, and soda together and let stand while creaming shortening and brown sugar. Add eggs. Sift dry ingredients and add to creamed mixture. Add applesauce to the mixture. Stir in nuts. Place in 9 x 13-inch flat pan and bake in slow oven at 275 degrees for 1 hour. Serves 12.

Sharon Robertson
Kansas City, Kansas

Cherry Cobbler

1 cup sugar
³/₄ cup flour
2 tsp. baking powder
Pinch of salt
²/₃ cup milk
4 tbsp. margarine
2 cups canned cherries, drained

Sift together sugar, flour, baking powder, and salt. Add milk, stir well. Melt margarine in 9 x 9-inch pan. Pour batter on top of melted margarine. Pour fruit on top of batter. Bake until brown at 350 degrees. Other fruits may be substituted. Serves 9.

Ann Porter
Pleasant Hill, Missouri

HEATH BAR CREAM TORTE

1 box white cake mix
2 cups whipping cream
16 oz. chocolate frosting
1 1/2 tsp. instant coffee
4 Heath candy bars,
   chopped

Prepare white cake mix as directed on box and bake in two 9-inch round pans. Cool and split each layer into two. Whip cream. Add chocolate frosting and coffee, blend well. Frost each layer of cake with 1/4 of the frosting and sprinkle with Heath candy bars. Serves 24.

Donna Maze
Roseburg, Oregon

HUCKLEBERRY CAKE

1 pt. whipping cream
2 tsp. vanilla
3 eggs
1 1/2 cups flour
1 1/2 cups sugar
2 tsp. baking powder
1/4 tsp. salt
1 1/2-2 cups fresh
   huckleberries (or
   frozen, thawed, and
   drained)

Beat cream until stiff, add vanilla. Beat eggs until thickened and fold into whipped cream. Mix together flour, sugar, baking powder, and salt. Fold dry ingredients into egg mixture. Then fold in huckleberries and pour into greased 9 x 13-inch pan. Bake at 350 degrees for about 45-60 minutes. Serves 9-12.

Linda Ward
Missoula, Montana

Dona Gene's Lemon Cake

I pkg. Duncan Hines
  Lemon Supreme
  cake mix
4 eggs
I pkg. lemon Jell-O
  (3 oz.)
³/₄ cup oil
³/₄ cup water

TOPPING:
2 cups sifted powdered
  sugar
¹/₂ cup fresh lemon juice

Mix cake mix, eggs, Jell-O, oil, and water together until smooth, about 2 minutes. Pour into 9 x 13-inch baking pan and bake at 350 degrees for 35 minutes.

TOPPING: Remove cake from oven and while still hot, use fork to poke the cake full of holes. Stir lemon juice and powdered sugar together until sugar dissolves and pour over the hot cake. This mixture soaks into the cake for a tasty treat. Serves 9-12.

Sharon Robertson
Kansas City, Kansas

JEWISH APPLE CAKE

3 cups flour
2 cups sugar
I cup salad oil
4 eggs
¹/₂ cup orange juice
2¹/₂ tsp. vanilla
3 tsp. baking powder
I tsp. salt
3 large apples, peeled
   and sliced

SUGAR MIXTURE:
¹/₂ cup sugar
I tsp. cinnamon
¹/₂ tsp. nutmeg

Place first 8 ingredients into bowl in order given. Beat until smooth. Place half of batter into greased and floured tube pan. Arrange apple slices on top of batter. Stir together sugar mixture and sprinkle half of it on batter. Repeat by adding the other half of the batter, remaining apple slices, and sugar mixture. Bake at 325 degrees for 1¹/₂ hours. Serves 16.

Cathie Malison
Bordertown, New Jersey

CHOCOLATE TRUFFLE CAKE

16 oz. semi-sweet
chocolate

1/2 cup unsalted butter

1/2 tbsp. flour

1/2 tbsp. sugar

I tsp. hot water

4 eggs, separated,
plus I egg white

I cup Mendocino cream
(for frosting)

MENDOCINO CREAM:

1/3 cup sour cream

3 egg whites

2/3 cup heavy cream

2 tsp. finely grated
lemon zest

3 tbsp. Grand Marnier
or other orange
flavored liqueur

Preheat oven to 425 degrees. Grease bottom of 8-inch springform pan. In top of double boiler melt chocolate and butter together. Remove from heat and add flour, sugar, and hot water. Beat egg whites until frothy, then add egg yolks and beat lightly. Fold egg mixture into chocolate mixture. Pour mixture into springform pan and bake 15 minutes—and not more. The cake will look very undone in the middle but that is the way it should look. Cool completely.

Frost top of cake with a very thick, smooth layer of Mendocino cream. Refrigerate. Cut cake while cold, but try to let it stand at room temperature about 15 minutes before serving. As the cake cools, it sinks a bit in the middle—that's usual, the cream covers it. It is best made a day ahead; it also freezes well. Serves 8-10.

MENDOCINO CREAM: In a small bowl, stir the sour cream until smooth. In a separate chilled bowl, whip the egg whites until they just hold their shape. Continue beating, adding sugar gradually until whites are thick and hold a soft peak. Add to the sour cream. Whip cream until it holds a soft peak and carefully fold into sour cream-egg white mixture along with lemon zest and Grand Marnier. Store covered in refrigerator for up to 4 hours.

Audrey Naismith

SOURDOUGH CHOCOLATE CAKE

I cup thick sourdough
  starter
I cup sugar
$^1/_2$ cup shortening
2 eggs
I tsp. vanilla
I tsp. cinnamon
I cup evaporated milk
3 1-oz. squares semi-
  sweet chocolate,
  melted
$^1/_2$ tsp. salt
I $^1/_2$ tsp. soda
2 cups flour

Prepare a cup of thick sourdough starter the night before. Set in warm spot. Cream sugar and shortening until light and fluffy. Beat in eggs, one at a time. Stir in starter, milk, vanilla, cinnamon, and chocolate. Beat for two minutes. Blend salt, soda, and flour, sprinkle over batter and fold in gently. Add 1 tbsp. hot water to the starter to liquify it and fold it into the batter. Pour in greased and floured 8-inch square pan. Bake at 350 degrees for 35-40 minutes. Cool and frost. Serves 9.

Ann Porter
Pleasant Hill, Missouri

BÛCHE DE NOËL (CHRISTMAS LOG)

3 eggs
³/₄ cup white sugar
¹/₃ cup brown sugar
¹/₃ cup water
I tsp. vanilla
I cup flour
I tsp. baking powder
¹/₄ tsp. salt

FILLING:
I pkg. Jell-O vanilla
   pudding (6-oz.)
¹/₄ cup peanut butter
2 Butterfinger candy
   bars, crushed
Cool Whip

Line jelly roll pan with greased foil. Beat eggs about 7 minutes until thick and lemon colored. Slowly add sugars. On low speed, add water and vanilla. Fold in flour, baking powder, and salt. Spread in jelly roll pan. Bake at 375 degrees for 12 minutes. Invert onto towel sprinkled with powdered sugar. Remove foil and roll up lengthwise with towel. Let cool.

Prepare pudding according to directions. Add peanut butter to hot cooked pudding. Cool. Unroll cake roll. Spread with filling. Sprinkle 1 crushed Butterfinger on top. Roll back up (of course, without the towel). To serve, cut roll at a slant. Top with Cool Whip and remaining crushed Butterfingers. Serves 8.

Yvonne Decker
Libby, Montana

COLD-OVEN POUND CAKE

1 1/2 cups butter
1 pkg. cream cheese
   (8 oz.)
3 cups sugar
6 eggs
3 cups flour
2 tsp. baking powder
1 tsp. vanilla extract
1 tsp. lemon extract

Cream butter and cream cheese and add sugar. Add eggs one at a time, beating after each addition. Add flour, baking powder, and extracts. Pour into greased and floured tube pan. Put cake in cold oven and bake at 300 degrees for 1 1/2 hours or until done. Serves 8-10.

Pansy Bowen
Missoula, Montana

PUMPKIN LOG

3 eggs
1 tsp. soda
1 cup sugar
1/2 tsp. cinnamon
3/4 cup flour
2/3 cup cooked pumpkin
1/2 cup powdered sugar
1/2 cup walnuts, chopped

TOPPING:
2 tbsp. butter, softened
3/4 tsp. vanilla
8 oz. cream cheese
1 1/2 cups chopped
   walnuts
1 cup powdered sugar

Mix first 6 ingredients and turn out onto greased waxed paper on a 10 x 15-inch greased cookie sheet. Sprinkle with 1/2 cup walnuts. Bake 15 minutes at 375 degrees. Turn onto a terry cloth towel sprinkled with 1/2 cup powdered sugar. Let cool. Combine topping ingredients and spread over cake. Roll like a jelly roll. Wrap in foil, chill at least 2 hours. Cut into slices to serve. Serves 6-8.

Suzy Cunrod
Helena, Montana

PEANUT BRITTLE

2 cups sugar
I cup light corn syrup
¹/₂ cup water
¹/₈ tsp. salt
10 oz. fresh raw Spanish
   peanuts
I tsp. soda
I tsp. vanilla
I tbsp. butter

Combine sugar, syrup, and water in large heavy pan. Place over medium heat and stir until sugar dissolves. Cover and cook for 3 minutes. Remove cover and cook to soft-ball stage (234 degrees on the candy thermometer). Add peanuts, stirring frequently, and cook until brittle reaches hard-crack stage (300 degrees). Remove from heat, add remaining ingredients, stir, spread on well-greased 14 x 17-inch cookie sheet. Cool; break in pieces.

Ann Porter
Pleasant Hill, Missouri

CORN FLAKE CANDY

I cup sugar
I cup white syrup
¹/₂ cup whipping cream
5 cups corn flakes
I cup coconut, shredded
I cup nuts

Cook sugar, syrup, and cream to a soft-ball stage. Let cool somewhat before pouring over corn flakes. Add coconut and nuts. Drop by spoonfuls on waxed paper. Chill. Makes about 10 dozen.

Ann Porter
Pleasant Hill, Missouri

Tootsie Rolls

3 tbsp. butter or
  margarine
2 squares unsweetened
  baking chocolate
¹/₂ cup light Karo syrup
1 tsp. vanilla
³/₄ cup powdered milk—
  sift until not grainy
3 cups powdered sugar

Melt the butter and chocolate in microwave or in double boiler—then add the remaining ingredients. Knead until well mixed. Roll into long thin roll and cut as desired. For a sour burst of flavor substitute 1 pkg. of Kool-Aid for the chocolate.

Pansy Bowen
Missoula, Montana

Elk Drops (No-bake Oatmeal Cookies)

1 cup margarine
¹/₂ cup sugar
¹/₄ cup cocoa
1 tsp. vanilla
3 cups rolled oats,
  uncooked
¹/₂ cup peanut butter
  (optional)
¹/₂ cup cocoa mix
  (optional)

Put margarine, sugar, and cocoa in saucepan. Bring to boil and cook 1 minute. Remove from heat. Add oatmeal and optional ingredients if desired. Mix. Place tablespoon-sized drops on waxed paper. Let cool. Makes about 5 dozen.

Sandy Mumm
Olathe, Colorado

Walnut Coconut Oatmeal Chews

2 cups quick cooking
   oats
I cup brown sugar,
   packed
¹/₂ cup salad oil
¹/₂ tsp. salt
I tsp. vanilla
2 eggs, slightly beaten
³/₄ cup chopped walnuts
I cup coconut, shredded

Mix oats, sugar, and oil in a large bowl. Let stand several hours in refrigerator. Add remaining ingredients. Mix well. Drop from a spoon in small mounds onto a well-greased baking sheet and pat down slightly. Bake at 350 degrees for 8-10 minutes. Makes about 4 dozen.

Ann Porter
Pleasant Hill, Missouri

Peanut Butter Cookies

I cup peanut butter
¹/₂ cup margarine,
   softened
I cup brown sugar,
   packed
¹/₂ tsp. vanilla
I egg
³/₄ cup all purpose flour
³/₄ cup whole wheat flour
I tsp. baking powder
¹/₄ tsp. salt

Cream together peanut butter, margarine, and sugar until light and fluffy. Add vanilla and egg. Mix dry ingredients together and add to butter mixture. Mix well. Form into golf ball-sized balls and put on cookie sheet, flatten with fork or any desired utensil, but don't flatten too much. Bake in a 375-degree oven for 10-12 minutes. Makes about 3 dozen cookies.

Linda Ward
Missoula, Montana

COWBOY COOKIES

I cup butter or margarine
¹/₂ cup sugar
I¹/₂ cups brown sugar
2 eggs
2 cups flour
I tsp. baking soda
¹/₂ tsp. salt
I¹/₂ tsp. vanilla
2 cups rolled oats,
    uncooked
I cup flaked coconut or
    raisins
I pkg. chocolate chips
    (12 oz.)

Cream butter and sugars. Add eggs and beat well. Mix in remaining ingredients. Drop by teaspoonfuls onto a greased cookie sheet and bake at 350 degrees for about 15 minutes. Makes about 8 dozen.

Pansy Bowen
Missoula, Montana

ITALIAN BISCOTTI COOKIES

2 cups sugar
I cup butter
5 eggs
3 tbsp. anise seed
I tsp. anise extract
2 cups chopped walnuts
5 cups flour
I tbsp. baking powder
¹/₂ tsp. salt

Cream butter and sugar. Add eggs and beat well. Add anise. Mix together dry ingredients and add to sugar mixture. Blend well. Add nuts. Shape into 3-inch-wide loaves on greased cookie sheet. Bake at 375 degrees for 20 minutes. Let cool 5 minutes. Cut into fingers on a slant. Lay them flat on cookie sheet and bake an additional 15-20 minutes or until cookies are crunchy. These crunchy sweet cookies are great for after dinner with coffee. Also, if kept in an airtight container, they last for weeks. These are great to take along hunting, too! Makes 8-10 dozen.

Chet and Luci Friday
Sacramento, California

SUGAR COOKIES

2 cups sugar
2 cups butter
3 eggs
5 cups flour
1 tsp. soda
1 tsp. cream of tartar
$^1/_4$ tsp. salt

Cream sugar and butter. Add eggs. Blend remaining ingredients and add to creamed ingredients. Mix well. Chill 1 hour. Roll out a small amount of dough at a time, keeping the rest refrigerated. Roll $^1/_8$-inch thick on floured board. Cut with 3-inch cookie cutter. Bake at 350 degrees for 8-10 minutes. Makes about 8 dozen.

Ann Porter
Pleasant Hill, Missouri

WET SHOO-FLY PIE

2 pie shells, 9-inch,
    unbaked

LIQUID MIXTURE:
1 cup molasses
2 cups brown sugar
2 cups hot water
1 tsp. baking soda
1 egg

CRUMBS:
3 cups flour
1 cup brown sugar
$^1/_2$ cup shortening or
    margarine, softened

Mix together liquid ingredients and divide equally and pour into 2 unbaked pie shells. Mix flour, brown sugar, and shortening with a fork until crumbly. Then spread evenly on top of liquid. Bake at 350 degrees about 45 minutes. Makes two 9-inch pies.

Mae Berger
Pine Grove, Pennsylvania

FUDGE PECAN PIE

¹/₂ cup sugar
¹/₃ cup cocoa
¹/₃ cup flour, unsifted
¹/₄ tsp. salt
1¹/₄ cups light corn syrup
3 eggs
3 tbsp. butter or
   margarine, melted
1¹/₂ tsp. vanilla
¹/₂ cup pecans, chopped
9-inch unbaked pastry
   shell
Pecan halves

Combine first 8 ingredients in large mixer bowl. Beat 30 seconds on medium speed. Do not overbeat. Stir in chopped pecans. Pour into unbaked pastry shell. Bake at 350 degrees for 55-60 minutes. Immediately arrange pecan halves on top. Cool. (For fullest flavor, cover and let stand a day before serving.) Serves 8-10.

NOTE: For fudge walnut pie substitute dark corn syrup for light corn syrup, 1 tbsp. maple flavor for vanilla, and walnuts for pecans.

Sharon Robertson
Kansas City, Kansas

APPLE PIE

2 quarts apple cider
1 quart "good" brandy
Cinnamon sticks
Whole cloves
Spices to taste

Mix together. Let flavors age for as long as you can stand it.

Marian Hartman
Wofford Heights, California

ORANGE RAISIN PIE

2 cups raisins
2 cups orange juice
½ cup brown sugar, packed
2 tbsp. cornstarch
½ tsp. cinnamon
¼ tsp. salt
I tsp. vinegar
I tbsp. margarine
Pastry for double 9-inch crust

Combine raisins and orange juice; boil 5 minutes. Blend sugar, cornstarch, cinnamon, and salt. Add to raisins and cook until clear. Remove from heat. Stir in vinegar and margarine. Cool slightly. Pour into pie shell. Cover with top pastry or lattice strips. Bake at 425 degrees about 30 minutes or until golden brown. Serves 8.

Sharon Robertson
Kansas City, Kansas

DIRT PIE

I pkg. Oreo cookies (12 oz.)

FILLING:
4 tbsp. margarine
I cup powdered sugar
8 oz. cream cheese
2 pkgs. instant vanilla pudding (3½ oz. each)
3½ cups milk
I cup Cool Whip

GARNISH:
Gummy worms
Silk flowers

Process cookies in blender or food processor until they look like potting soil. Cream margarine, cream cheese, and powdered sugar. Mix milk, pudding, and Cool Whip together and add to creamed mixture. Layer soil (Oreo cookies), filling, soil, filling, soil, in 8-inch plastic flower pot. Decorate with gummy worms and silk flowers.

Dwayne Porter
Pleasant Hill, Missouri

CHERRIES IN THE SNOW

2 pkgs. cream cheese
  (8 oz. each)
I cup confectioner's
  sugar
I cup milk
I carton Cool Whip
  (12-oz.)
I angel food cake
I can cherry pie filling
  (16 oz.)

Break angel food cake into small pieces on serving dish. Mix cream cheese, sugar, and milk together until blended. Add Cool Whip. Add this mixture to angel food cake pieces. Mix. Spread cherry pie filling on top of mixture. Refrigerate. Serves 10.

Sharon Robertson
Kansas City, Kansas

JELL-O DESSERT

Angel food cake
3 pkg. wild strawberry
  Jell-O (3 oz. each)
3 cups hot water
¹/₂ cup sugar
2 pkgs. frozen
  strawberries, partially
  thawed (10 oz. each)
I pt. whipping cream
  (or light Cool Whip)

Break half of angel food cake into small pieces and spread over bottom of 9 x 13-inch pan. Set aside. Dissolve Jell-O in water. Add sugar and then the frozen strawberries. Stir until strawberries are broken up. Whip cream and add to Jell-O mixture. A wire whip is best for mixing. Pour Jell-O mixture over the cake pieces. Be sure cake pieces are covered. Chill until set. Serves 9-12.

Linda Padgett
Washougal, Washington

BLUEBERRY BUCKLE

³/₄ cup sugar
¹/₄ cup soft shortening
I egg
¹/₂ cup milk
2 cups sifted flour
2 tsp. baking powder
¹/₂ tsp. salt
2 cups blueberries,
    drained

CRUMB TOPPING:
¹/₂ cup sugar
¹/₃ cup sifted flour
¹/₂ tsp. cinnamon
¹/₄ cup soft butter

Mix sugar, shortening, and egg together thoroughly. Stir in ¹/₂ cup milk. Sift together flour, baking powder, and salt and stir. Blend in blueberries. Spread batter in 9-inch square greased and floured pan. Mix together crumb topping ingredients and sprinkle over batter. Bake 45-50 minutes at 375 degrees. Serves 9.

Cathie Malison
Bordentown, New Jersey

CARAMEL DUMPLINGS

CAKE BATTER:
¹/₂ cup sugar
Butter, size of an egg
¹/₂ cup milk
I tsp. vanilla
I tsp. baking powder
White flour

CARAMEL:
¹/₂ cup brown sugar
2¹/₂ cups boiling water
I cup white sugar
I tbsp. butter

Prepare cake batter by creaming butter and sugar. Add milk, vanilla, and baking powder. Add enough flour to make a stiff batter. Combine caramel ingredients and boil for 10 minutes. Drop batter by spoonfuls into caramel and boil 15 mintues.

Ann Porter
Pleasant Hill, Missouri

Ice Cream

12 eggs
4 cups whipping cream
14 oz. sweetened,
    condensed milk
1 tsp. vanilla
1 cup sugar
2 cups milk

Mix and put in ice cream freezer. Pack with ice and salt and turn that crank! Desired consistency should be reached in 15-45 minutes.

Ann Porter
Pleasant Hill, Missouri

Stir Crazy Cake

2$\frac{1}{2}$ cups flour
1$\frac{1}{2}$ cups sugar
$\frac{1}{2}$ cup cocoa
2 tsp. soda
$\frac{1}{2}$ tsp. salt
$\frac{2}{3}$ cup oil
2 tbsp. vinegar
1 tbsp. vanilla
2 cups cold coffee
$\frac{1}{4}$ cup sugar
$\frac{1}{2}$ tsp. cinnamon

Put first 5 ingredients in ungreased 13 x 9-inch pan. Stir with fork to mix. Form 3 wells in flour mixture. Pour oil in 1 well, vinegar in the next, and vanilla in last well. Pour coffee over all and stir with fork until well mixed. Do not beat. Combine remaining sugar and cinnamon. Sprinkle over batter. Bake at 350 degrees for 35-40 minutes. Serves 12.

Evelyn Kinsey

GRANOLA

4 cups rolled oats
1½ cups wheat germ
¾ cup sunflower seeds
   (4 oz.)
1 pkg. slivered almonds
   (7 oz.)
¾ cup coconut, shredded
¾ cup cooking oil
1 cup honey
2 tbsp. milk
2 tsp. vanilla

Mix together first 5 ingredients. Warm remaining ingredients in saucepan. Mix all ingredients together; spread on a cookie sheet or roasting pan. Bake in 250-degree oven for about 1 hour, stirring occasionally. Makes about 7 cups.

Paul T. Robinson
Providence, Utah

CAMP COOKING

Dutch Oven Chix Wings

**2 large pkgs. frozen
  chicken wings (3 lbs.)**
**1 bottle Heinz 57 sauce
  (12 oz.)**
2 tbsp. butter
2 tsp. dry mustard
**1 bottle soy sauce
  (5 oz.)**
**2 tbsp. Worcestershire
  sauce**
**3 bottles Louisiana
  hot sauce (2 oz.)**
³/₄ cup brown sugar

Place chicken wings in Dutch oven. Add remaining ingredients—you may adjust measurements to taste. Cover and simmer over low fire for 2 hours. Makes about 60 wings.

Shawn Eichelberger
Phoenix, Arizona

Elk Salami Tidbits

**1 medium onion,
  chopped**
**1¹/₂ tbsp. butter or
  margarine**
**12 oz. good-quality chili
  sauce**
6 oz. water
¹/₂ tbsp. lemon juice
4 oz. brown sugar
**3 drops to ¹/₂ tsp.
  Tabasco sauce**
1 lb. elk salami

Slice salami into ¹/₈-inch slices. Sauté onion in butter. Add everything except salami. Simmer until mixture is thickened. Arrange salami slices in a single layer in a large, shallow, foil-lined baking dish. Pour sauce over salami and let stand 2 hours. Bake in preheated 300-degree oven, basting and turning frequently. Serve with crackers, bread, mustard, and any leftover sauce. Serves 12.

NOTE: See Ron Sunberg's Mandarin Grouse recipe for hints on how to bake at camp.

Linda Ward
Missoula, Montana

Yeast Roll Delight

2 cups lukewarm water
¹/₂ cup sugar
1¹/₂ tsp. salt
2 cakes compressed
**   yeast**
1 egg
¹/₄ cup shortening
6¹/₂-7 cups unbleached
**   flour**

Dissolve yeast in ¹/₂ cup lukewarm water and set aside for 5 minutes. In large bowl combine remaining water, sugar, and salt. Add yeast and then egg and shortening. Mix in flour first with spoon, then with hand. Do not knead. Shape dough into desired roll shapes. Cover and let rise until light (1¹/₂-2 hours). Bake on greased cookie sheet at 400 degrees for 10-12 minutes.

These are delicious. At camp, I use my Dutch oven. Leftovers can be used for deli sandwich fixings for the next day's lunch in the woods. Makes about 3-3¹/₂ dozen.

Linda Padgett
Washougal, Washington

Glazed Potato Doughnuts

I pkg. yeast
¹/₄ cup warm water
**I cup milk, scalded
(use powdered milk
at camp)**
¹/₄ cup oil
¹/₄ cup sugar
I tsp. salt
**³/₄ cup mashed potatoes
(leftovers from the
night before; can also
use instant)**
2 eggs, beaten
5-6 cups flour
I lb. powdered sugar
6 tbsp. water
I tbsp. vanilla
Oil for deep fat frying

Dissolve yeast in warm water. In a large bowl, combine milk, oil, sugar, and salt. Cool until lukewarm. Stir in yeast, potatoes, and eggs. Gradually add enough flour to make soft dough. Knead on unfloured board until smooth. Place in lightly greased bowl. Cover and let rise 1-1¹/₂ hours in warm place. Roll to ¹/₂-inch thickness, cut with 3-inch doughnut cutter. Place flat on baking, sheet. Cover. Let rise until double, about 30 minutes. Deep-fat fry doughnuts in hot oil. My Dutch oven worked great for this. Drain on absorbent paper.

For glaze, stir powdered sugar, water and vanilla together. (Mixture should look like thick cream). Swirl hot doughnuts in glaze. Place on cooling rack until glaze is set. Additions to glaze might be coconut, chocolate, or maple. Makes about 4 dozen.

Linda Padgett
Washougal, Washington

Camp Onions

Beef bouillon granules
Onions, as many as you like

Peel and quarter onions. Sprinkle beef bouillon granules on top. Wrap in foil and throw on the grill. Roll the onions around and when soft to the squeeze, they are done. Do an extra onion to chop and mix with the scrambled eggs in the morning!

Jack Lutch
Wickenburg, Arizona

Camp Beans 101

2 lbs. elk burger
A bowl full of chopped onion
Green peppers, chopped
Mushrooms, sliced
Black and green olives
2 large cans of pork and beans (28 oz. each)
1 small can of tomato paste (6 oz.)
1 can tomato sauce (8 oz.)
2 tbsp. molasses
Brown sugar to taste
Garlic powder to taste
Salt and pepper to taste
Anything else you care to add

After browning the meat, I just dump it all together in a large cast iron pot with a lid and simmer. Serves 12-15.

Rick Anzalone
Chehalis, Washington

Baked Stuffed Mandarin Grouse a la Ron

**One large tender grouse
  per hunter**
**2 cans mandarin oranges
  (8 oz. each) per
  grouse**
Bread for stuffing
Salt and pepper

Clean and skin grouse and soak in ice-cold alpine lake (7,000 ft. or higher) water. Tap water will suffice if necessary. Salt and pepper inside of body cavity. Rub it in good with your fingers and then stuff with torn-up pieces of bread. Place stuffed grouse breast-side down in smallest pan with lid into which they will fit. Mash mandarin orange segments (squish between your fingers) and pour segments and juice over the grouse. While it is not necessary to completely cover the grouse, the mandarin sauce should nearly cover it. Cover and bake for 1¹/₂ hours at 350 degrees.

If in a wall tent, place 3 metal spoons upside down on medium hot wood stove top, place covered pan with grouse in it on top of spoons. Then place your biggest pan upside down over the entire contraption. This works as an oven.

Ron Sundberg
Olympia, Washington

GROUSE AU GRATIN

HOME VERSION:

Any legal grouse,
   skinned, filleted,
   and cubed
4 medium potatoes,
   peeled and sliced
I cup grated cheddar
   cheese
2¹/₂ cups milk
¹/₄ cup flour
¹/₄ cup butter or
   margarine
¹/₄ cup diced onions
I tsp. dried parsley
   flakes
¹/₄ tsp. garlic powder

CAMP VERSION:

Any legal grouse,
   filleted, skinned,
   and cubed
Your choice of boxed
   au gratin potatoes
Butter
Seasonings

HOME VERSION: Cook onion in butter or margarine until tender. Stir in flour, let cook a few minutes, and then add milk. Cook and stir until thickened. Layer potatoes in a 2-quart casserole dish. Lightly brown grouse in butter and season with garlic powder. Add to layer of potatoes. Sprinkle parsley on potatoes and grouse, pour onion sauce over. Spread cheese on top; then bake covered at 350 degrees for 45 minutes or microwave on high for 15-25 minutes. Serves 2-4.

CAMP VERSION: Brown the cubed grouse with a dash of salt, pepper, and garlic (if available). Add the browned cubes to the ingredients contained in the boxed potatoes. Follow directions on the box, except cook over fire until done. You may substitute partridge or pheasant for grouse. Serves 2-4.

Douglas Nott
Yakima, Washington

Game Bird Nuggets

**Breasts of quail,
    pheasant, snipe,
    dove, etc.**
Salt and pepper to taste
Flour
Margarine

Bone breasts. Cut into large bite-sized pieces. Salt and pepper them to taste. Put several tablespoons of flour into a paper bag, and shake the bird pieces until coated. Heat margarine (approximately 2 tbsp. per four birds) in a frying pan. Add the bird nuggets and fry until just brown on outside; don't overcook. Set aside and keep warm. Make gravy from the drippings. This works well with duck also, and is a solution to those birds that may be a little shot up!

*Jo Bigman
Gold Hill, Oregon*

CARIBOU-ELK FOIL SPECIAL

1 lb. ground elk or
  caribou
10 slices bacon
3 carrots, chopped
3 potatoes, chopped
1 large onion, chopped
1 tsp. each salt, pepper,
  and garlic powder

Place 5 slices of bacon on foil, dull side out, then add half of the carrots, onions, and potatoes on top. Add spices to meat and put on top. Add remaining vegetables and bacon and close tightly. Lay on hot coals for 30 minutes on each side. Serves 4.

Sharon Robertson
Kansas City, Kansas

CAMPFIRE BLACK POT STEW

4 lb. eye of round elk
   roast (or beef)
Flour, salt, and pepper
4 medium onions,
   peeled and quartered
4 red potatoes, peeled
   and quartered
2 large carrots, scraped
   and cut into 4-inch
   lengths
1 green pepper, chopped
2 cans beef bouillon
   (10 oz. each)
1 cup red wine
   (optional)
$1/2$ tsp. each dried
   oregano, thyme, basil,
   and garlic powder

EQUIPMENT:
One 12-inch Dutch oven
   with legs
Shovel, ax, pot holders
   (or 2 shirttails)
Paper towels

THE FIRE: You need good ashes hot enough to make your hand smart. Usually a 3-day fire is enough. Dig a hole one foot down into the fire pit. Put 2 shovels of hot ashes in the bottom of the hole. Place the open oven over the coals.

THE STEW: Dredge roast in flour, salt, and pepper and brown in small amount of oil in hot oven. Remove and set aside. Add more oil and brown onions. Arrange browned roast on top of onions. Add potatoes, carrots, and green pepper. Add beef bouillon, red wine, and spices. You must add enough water to completely cover the ingredients in the pot. Cover the pot and mark which way the handle is laying so you can lift it out later. Put two good shovels of cold dirt on top of pot. Cover pot with hot ashes and then keep a small fire going for 8-10 hours. Dig out the pot. Sweep off ashes and enjoy. Serves 8-10.

De Bunijs
Sierra Vista, Arizona

Barbecue Sauce

1 cup ketchup
4 tbsp. brown sugar
¹/₂ cup white vinegar
4 tbsp. Worcestershire
    sauce
2 tsp. celery seed
1 tsp. chili powder
1 tsp. seasoned salt

Mix all ingredients with wire whisk. Spread on ribs or other meat prior to cooking. Makes 1³/₄ cups.

Connie Elliot

Mustard Glaze Barbecue Sauce

¹/₂ cup prepared mustard
¹/₃ cup cider vinegar or
    lemon juice
¹/₃ cup packed light
    brown sugar
¹/₂ cup honey
1 tbsp. soy sauce
1 tbsp. oil

Whisk together all ingredients, simmer and stir for 5 minutes. Good on elk roast, ribs, and lamb. Makes 1¹/₄ cups.

Salle Rice
Butte, Montana

Missouri River Grilled Trout

1 large trout, cleaned
  and rinsed
Lemon pepper to taste
1 cup cooked rice
Corn husks
2 tbsp. butter
¹/₄ tsp. parsley flakes
¹/₄ tsp. garlic powder
¹/₄ tsp. onion powder
¹/₂ tsp. lemon juice
1 drop Liquid Smoke
1 tsp. Worcestershire
  sauce

Sprinkle inside of trout with lemon pepper and stuff belly with rice. Wrap trout in corn husks and place on large sheet of aluminum foil. Melt butter and mix well with remaining ingredients. Pour over corn husks. Wrap foil around fish loosely but so that sauce cannot escape. Place wrapped trout over red-hot barbecue coals or campfire and grill 10 minutes on each side. Trout should flake easily when done.

Mr. and Mrs. R. S. Yaeger
Helena, Montana

SMOKING AND CURING YOUR OWN FISH

Smoking brined fish is an ancient technique that not only preserves your catch, but also turns it into a delicacy. A measure of its value is the price smoked fish commands in the market. Yet, with just a few hours' time and minimal equipment, you can produce it at home.

To begin, clean and scale the fish. Use small trout or mackerel whole, fillet larger fish (cut in half lengthwise and discard backbone, but do not skin). Or use 1-1¹/₂-inch thick steaks.

Step two is to cure the fish, either by soaking it in a brine or by packing it in a dry cure. We give directions for both on the following pages. Although we found it easier to control the amount of salt penetration and the moistness of the finished fish with wet brine, the dry mixture, which requires no pans, is an easy way to cure and smoke fish at your fishing site. Each curing mixture makes enough to cure 10 pounds of fish.

Smoking, the third step, can be done on any type of covered barbecue (including commercial smokers). Only the size of the grill determines how many fish you can smoke. Cooked slowly over a low heat that's carefully monitored with an oven thermometer, the fish stays moist and has time to absorb the swirling smoke of the wood chips. Almost any type of fish can be smoked, but fatty types such as salmon, steelhead, trout, sturgeon, sablefish (or butterfish), albacore, and mackerel retain a more moist texture. Striped bass, moderately low in fat, is also excellent. Serve smoked fish warm or at room temperature as an entrée, an appetizer, or for breakfast. The flavor is quite rich, so portions can be modest.

Les Roberts
Eugene, Oregon

WET BRINE CURE

3 qts. cold water
1½ cups salt
¾ cup brown sugar,
    firmly packed
1½ cups sugar
1 tbsp. white
    peppercorns
6 bay leaves
1½ tsp. whole allspice
1½ tsp. whole cloves
1 tsp. ground dried
    ginger
1 clove garlic, peeled
    and split

In a noncorrodible container (such as glass or stainless steel) just large enough to hold your fish, combine all ingredients and stir briskly until salt and sugar dissolve. Add fish to brine, making sure all surfaces are covered (if fish floats, turn skin side up so flesh is submerged). Cover and let stand at room temperature 2 hours or in the refrigerator as long as 6 hours. Cures 10 lbs.

Les Roberts
Eugene, Oregon

DRY PACK CURE

SALT MIXTURE:

1 cup rock salt

1 cup brown sugar,
   firmly packed

3/4 tsp. ground white
   pepper

1 1/2 tsp. ground allspice

1 1/2 tsp. ground dried
   ginger

1/2 tsp. cracked bay leaf

1 clove garlic, minced or
   pressed

In a large container, mix salt mixture ingredients. Arrange sheets of waxed paper on a flat surface. Sprinkle about 1/3 of salt mixture in center of paper and set fish skin side down on top. Pat remaining mixture into flesh. Cover and let stand at room temperature 2 hours or in the refrigerator as long as 6 hours.

After curing, lift fish from wet or dry salt mixture; rinse thoroughly under a slow stream of cold water, gently rubbing flesh, if necessary, to release salt. Place fish skin side down on several layers of paper towels. Blot to dry. Let dry uncovered at room temperature until flesh feels tacky, about 30 minutes.

Les Roberts
Eugene, Oregon

SMOKING

SYRUP BASTE:
1/3 **cup maple-flavored syrup**
1 1/2 **tbsp. soy sauce**
1/4 **tsp. ground dried ginger**

Stir together syrup baste. Set aside. Ignite 20 charcoal briquets on the firebed of your barbecue. Cover about 4 cups of hickory chips with water; let stand at least 20 minutes. When the coals are completely covered with gray ash (about 30 minutes), push 6 coals to each side of firebed in a medium-size (22-inch diameter) covered barbecue, 5 coals to each side in a small (18-inch diameter) barbecue, and about 8 coals to each side in a large (26-inch diameter or 19 x 33-inch rectangle) barbecue. Transfer any remaining coals to another barbecue or metal pan; add 4-6 new coals so they'll ignite for later use. Grease grill. For fish fillets, lightly grease skin to prevent sticking. Drain wood chips; sprinkle about 1/2 cup over each half of the hot coals in barbecue. Set grill about 6 inches above coals. Position fish (skin side down for filets) side by side on center of grill so no part extends over coals. Place oven thermometer in center of grill on top of fish if necessary. Put hood over grill. If barbecue is vented, adjust to maintain low heat (check manufacturer's directions). When fish has smoked about 20 minutes, check thermometer; it should read 160-180 degrees. If temperature drops below 160 degrees, add 1-2 coals to each side of barbecue (remove 1-2 coals if too hot). Sprinkle each pile of coals with an additional 1/2 cup wet hickory chips. Pat surface of fish with a paper towel to keep dry; brush lightly with syrup baste. Continue smoke-cooking until fish flakes when prodded with a fork in thickest portion; it takes about 1 hour for small fish, 2-3 hours for 1-1 1/2-inch thick fish fillets or steaks. To remove fish from grill, loosen edges with a wide spatula, if necessary, then slide gently onto a rimless baking sheet; serve hot or let cool to room temperature. To store, wrap airtight and refrigerate as long as 2 weeks, or freeze up to 6 months; thaw to serve.

Les Roberts
Eugene, Oregon

Fish Brine

This is another variation on a wet brine cure.

- **1 cup soy sauce**
- **1 cup apple wine, cider, or apple juice**
- **¼ cup salt**
- **½ cup brown sugar**
- **½ tsp. garlic salt**
- **½ tsp. onion salt**
- **½ tsp. black pepper**

Mix brine ingredients together. Clean salmon or steelhead, rubbing it well with dry salt to get rid of blood, grit, loose membrane, and other unwanted material. Rinse in cold, fresh water. Drop chunks of fish into brine and leave overnight in refrigerator, about 20 hours or so. Remove and dry thoroughly with paper towels, but do not rinse. Put immediately into smoker and smoke for 8-10 hours. Brine covers 1 fish.

Cheryl Hall
West Linn, Oregon

A Hodgepodge of Meat Care

by David Stalling

> *"Any marksman can kill game. But killing is merely a part of the hunting experience, perhaps the easiest. It's the difficulties between kill and kitchen that separate the shooter from the hunter. The finest chef can't undo damage wreaked by sloppy field handling."*
>
> —Jack McCready
> *Furred and Feathered Wild Game from Bullet to Table*

If you worry about how you're gonna get an elk out of the mountains before you shoot it, you won't be a good elk hunter. At least that's the advice I once got from an old timer. A pretty tough old timer. And there's some truth to it. But the first time I killed an elk in a jackstrawed spruce bottom several steep, doghaired miles from the trail, I questioned that wisdom. And with the early September sun quickly warming, I worried how my year's supply of meat would taste if I didn't cool it and get it out fast. I didn't. And lost some fine meat.

Not an uncommon experience. In fact, some state fish and game agencies estimate up to 70 percent of wild game meat spoils through poor field handling. Marty Auch, a butcher and owner of Hamilton Packing in Montana's Bitterroot Valley, processes more than 300 elk a year. He sees a lot of wasted meat. Why? Poor shots, where recovering game took a long time and meat rotted around bullet holes; failure to cool meat quickly and properly; not keeping meat free of dirt, pine needles, and flies; and aging meat too long. Not that you can't shoot an elk in some steep, dense basin far from roads and trails and still have fine meat—you just need to be prepared and know what kind of job you're in for.

Most hunters are fairly free with advice and opinions. And advice on field dressing elk and caring for meat varies nearly as much as opinions on what's the best cartridge for elk. But all agree on this: what you do the first several hours after killing an elk will affect the quality of meat you'll be eating the rest of the year. If cared for properly, nothing tastes as fine as elk; if not, it can be as savory and tender as an old hunting boot. While techniques for proper game care differ, there are some basic rules: the three major things that cause meat to spoil are dirt, heat, and moisture. So the best way to ensure high-quality meat is to make a quick, clean kill, gut the elk immediately, cool the meat, keep it cool, and keep it clean. The more careful you are, the better the elk will taste.

THE KILL

Hasty shots often result in wounded, slow-dying elk . . . and long searches to find the carcass. An elk's chemical balance changes when it's shot—adrenaline and enzymes pumped into the bloodstream spoil meat. So does a shot to the guts. And the harder it is to find a dead elk, the longer the carcass will maintain heat and body fluids. We all strive for a quick, clean kill out of respect for the animals we hunt—but such kills also allow us to quickly gut an elk, cool the carcass, and ensure high-quality meat.

THE TOOLS

When you kill, the fun of the hunt is over and the work begins. So some folks say. And there's some truth to it, too. Few tasks are as intimidating as the prospect of getting a 600-pound elk out of the backcountry. By breaking the job down into small tasks, it becomes more manageable. And fun, too. Sort of.

Field dressing reduces a 600-pound elk to 400. Removing the head and hide shaves another 50 pounds. And if you bone out all the meat, you'll only have about 170 pounds to carry—several trips with a strong back, a good packboard, and a few *really* nice friends.

Like most jobs, it's much easier and more pleasant with proper tools. Here's a list of the basics: nylon cord, several sharp knives, steel or stone for sharpening knives, a folding saw or hatchet, a towel, game bags, a small bag for the heart and liver, and a flashlight with extra batteries—in case you're tracking and field dressing after dark. A light tarp, space blanket, or poncho comes in handy to keep meat out of the dirt.

BLEED IT?

If meat sits too long in blood, it will spoil. But hunters disagree on whether to bleed an elk, a common practice a generation ago. Some hunters say since a dead elk's heart no longer pumps blood, it's enough to gut the animal, drain blood from the chest cavity and wipe the cavity clean. Others say the network of small arteries and veins throughout an elk's body remains filled with blood which can taint the meat. They favor cutting the elk's jugular—or other major veins or arteries if you're preserving the cape. Basically, it's a matter of preference.

FIELD DRESSING

Hunters also haggle over whether it's best to gut an elk from front to back, or back to front. No matter—as long as you remove the entrails as quickly as possible without puncturing them, and without getting hair and body fluids on the meat. Here's a common, straightforward approach:

1) Roll the elk on its back, tying the legs out of the way with cord or rope.

2) With your knife, make an incision through the elk's hide near the anus.

3) Lifting with the knife in one hand, while using the other hand to push the intestines and stomach out of the way, cut through the hide all the way up to the breast bone. *Do not puncture the internal organs.* Cut around the sex organs. In many states, sex organs must be left attached to the carcass.

4) Hold the entrails down with one hand, and keeping your knife along the rib cage, cut the diaphragm—a membrane separating the lung and heart area from the stomach, paunch, and intestines. The diaphragm attaches the internal organs to the rib cage and needs to be cut so the entrails can be removed.

5) Cut through the hide above the breast bone and continue cutting up the neck to the chin. (If you plan to mount the head or tan the hide, you need to skin and cape the animal before cutting along the neck.) Some hunters use a saw or hatchet to split the breast bone and open the carcass up even more. Cut the windpipe and esophagus at the upper neck and tie them off with cord. An elk's windpipe and esophagus sour quickly and will taint meat if not removed.

6) Keeping your knife close to the pelvic bone, cut a circle around the anus and tie off the intestines, keeping excrement from spilling on the meat. Some folks use a saw or hatchet to cut through the pelvic bone and open the animal up even more.

7) Reach up into the chest cavity and grab the windpipe and esophagus. Carefully work loose the internal organs and slide them out of the animal. It helps to have the rear of the animal facing downhill. If you like the heart and liver, cut them out before you slide the entrails into the dirt. Put them in a small bag to keep them clean and out of reach of birds and insects.

8) Drain the body cavity, clean it, and dry it with a towel and prop it open with a stick. Some hunters leave their elk at this stage, to return later with help. But the carcass cools faster if you bone or quarter it.

TO SKIN OR NOT TO SKIN?

The thick hide of an elk can serve as the best game bag around, keeping meat clean and preventing spoilage. So a lot of hunters don't skin the carcass until they get home where conditions are cleaner. But skin can also seal heat in, preventing meat from cooling—particularly during warm, early hunting seasons. And it's easier to skin an elk while it's still warm. So what do you do?

It depends. Auch says if it's warm and you can keep the meat clean, go ahead and skin it. Otherwise, leave it on. The risks of getting hair, dirt, and pine needles all over the meat outweigh the benefits of cooling the elk quicker.

COOL IT—AND KEEP IT COOL

The best way to cool an elk is to cut it up and hang it in a cool place where air can circulate around it. How far you go in cutting the elk up depends on how you plan to pack it out. If close enough to a road, some folks drag their elk out whole—although dragging elk over rocks and logs can bruise a lot of meat. Quartering is the most common method.

To quarter an elk, split the carcass down the backbone with a saw or hatchet, then cut each length in half between the first and second ribs, counting in from the back. Cut the legs off at the joints, then hang the quarters in a shady spot. If you can't hang the elk, prop it up against a log or rock so air can circulate all around it.

A horse can easily pack two elk quarters. And, with a little sweat and hard work, a healthy person can carry a quarter. But if you have a long hike ahead, it's best to cut the elk up even further. There's no sense in carrying a lot of bone. Be sure to spread the meat out and cool it before you throw it all in a bag. Auch says he has seen elk ruined by hunters who boned the meat and immediately piled it all in a game bag without letting it cool. Even during late, cold November hunts, meat can spoil from internal body heat if an elk is not opened and cooled quickly enough.

KEEP IT CLEAN

As elk meat is cut and quartered, it should be placed in a breathable game bag to keep flies and birds from getting to it. Some old-timers carry a can of black pepper with them, and sprinkle it on the meat to protect it from marauders. It works, but it's not necessary if you have good game bags. While cutting up elk, it's very important to keep meat clean and dry. Dirt introduces bacteria that sours meat. Moisture, including blood and water, enhances bacterial growth, speeding up spoilage. Where meat can air dry, it's all right to clean it with snow or water, but it shouldn't sit in constant contact with moisture. Bloodshot areas around bullet or arrow wounds should also be cut off and cleaned to prevent bacteria from spreading. Once they get their elk home, many hunters hang the meat and wipe it clean with a mixture of vinegar and water.

AGING

Aging an elk allows natural enzymes to tenderize the meat. Under ideal conditions where temperature and humidity are constant—like in a meat processing plant—elk can age for several weeks. But most elk are shot in less-than-ideal places, where dirt, hair, and heat take their toll. If bacteria has already begun to spoil meat, hanging it can make things worse. Auch recommends hanging an elk for about 10 days, in a dry, cool place, if temperatures can be kept constant at about 38 degrees. If temperatures are below freezing, or much warmer than 40 degrees, it's best to get the meat into a controlled cooler.

BUTCHERING

Some hunters pay professional butchers to cut their meat. Others prefer to do it on their own. If you do it yourself, it helps to have the proper tools: a solid table or work bench, a good cutting board, several sharp knives, a meat saw, and a cleaver. As you cut up the meat, clean off clots of blood, hair, dirt, and damaged meat. A towel soaked in vinegar works well for this. Fat should also be trimmed, as it can make meat taste rancid. Meat that is chilled—but not frozen— is easier to cut than warm meat. The following chart shows basic cuts of an elk, and the most common uses of each cut:

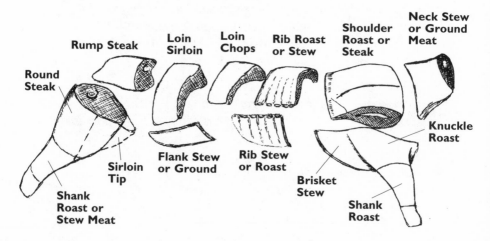

FREEZING

Good freezer wrap is essential. As you wrap meat, force air out and wrap tightly to create an airtight seal. Double wrapping helps prevent freezer burn. Label and date each package and freeze it rapidly at about 10 degrees below zero—or the lowest setting on your freezer. Packages should be scattered, if possible, so each one cools and freezes quickly.

COOKING

Since elk meat is far leaner than domestic beef, many folks overcook it, leaving it parched and leathery. Adding bacon strips or fat while cooking elk can help keep it moist. Marinades, tenderizers, and seasonings enhance taste and moistness.

One of the more rewarding aspects of hunting is eating the meat you've brought home and prepared. For many of us, it's the closest and most personal way to partake of an older, more natural way of life. If you treat an elk carefully and properly after making a quick, clean kill, you will end up with the finest tasting meat in the world.

INDEX